MYTHS and MIRACLES

A new approach to Genesis 1~11

David C. C. Watson

Disclaimer

Page 36 of this book, *Myths and Miracles*, mentions the Paluxy footprints. Many extremely human-like prints were found alongside those of dinosaurs at this site. Creationist scientists have now advised extreme caution in regarding these as definitely human, pending further research. This is because a curious reddish stain appeared around some of these tracks in a three-pronged pattern. Such patterns are characteristic of certain types of dinosaurs. It should be stressed that the stain was not an actual indentation in the rock.

CREATION SCIENCE FOUNDATION LTD

215

This reprint published by
Creation Science Foundation Ltd,
(Incorporated in Queensland),
P.O. Box 302, Sunnybank,
Qld, 4109 Australia

Phone: (07) 345 8122 [International: +617 345 8122]
Fax: (07) 345 3887 [International: +617 345 3887]

(First edition published by H.E. Walter Ltd, Sussex, England.)

First Australian printing, 1988

ISBN 0 85479 601 0

Printed in Australia by Watson Ferguson and Co., Brisbane

To the schools and scholars of Great Britain

'Give instruction to a wise man, and he will be still wiser'.

Proverbs 9.9.

ABBREVIATIONS

AV	Authorized Version
CLC	Christian Literature Crusade
CRS (Q)	Creation Research Society (Quarterly)
EB	Encyclopaedia Britannica
EPM	Evolution Protest Movement
GBR	Guinness Book of Records
RE	Religious Education
RSV	Revised Standard Version (of the Bible)
STL	Send The Light
TOE	Theory of Evolution
WBE	World Books Encyclopaedia
WTP	The World That Perished (No. 3 in Bibliography)

Note: Throughout this book the word 'myth' is used to mean a *widespread but mistaken idea, a popular fallacy;* except in chs. 2 and 9, where the difference is noted.

ACKNOWLEDGEMENTS

It seems an impertinence to thank Brian Newton for his superb illustrations, because anyone can see that this book is as much his as mine. However, it should be mentioned that he made time to draw them in less than six months, in spite of being fully occupied as a teacher in Geography. I am most grateful to him, and also to Bruce Baker, who reviewed nearly the whole text and made valuable suggestions and corrections. Further corrections and suggestions will always be welcomed by

> D.C.C.W.
> Creation Science Movement (UK)
> 50 Brecon Avenue,
> Cosham, Portsmouth, P06 2AW,
> ENGLAND

CONTENTS

INTRODUCTION

'WHAT SHALL WE TEACH THE CHILDREN?' about Genesis 1—11 has perplexed at least three generations of Scripture teachers. One popular answer is: 'I always start with Abraham!' But is this right, or necessary?

In these pages the author of 'The Great Brain Robbery' cuts the Gordian knot by proposing that

(a) nothing stated in those ancient records is contrary to the established *facts* of science or history;

(b) many facts of science and history agree far better with the Bible account of a literal six-day creation dated only thousands of years ago, followed by a world-wide Flood, than with the fragile hypotheses and fabulous aeons of Evolution.

Much of the source-material for this book is American. America gave the world Dwight L. Moody, the Auca martyrs and Billy Graham. She has now given us another example of Christian leadership in the formation of the Creation Research Society (1963), the Bible-Science Association, and the Institute for Creation Research at San Diego. It is hoped that this little book may lead more Christians in Britain to acknowledge the debt we owe them, just as William Tyndale and John Knox were glad to receive help and guidance from the great European masters of the Reformation.

In a school textbook it is pointless to give detailed references to source-material, but RE Teachers would be well-advised to study and stock their libraries with five or six of the books listed in the Bibliography. These represent but a fraction of the vast amount of creationist literature and AV material produced since 1960. (The Bible-Science Association catalogue lists some 1200 books, pamphlets, filmstrips etc.).

Deliberately I have ignored critical questions (except in Appendix B), because they have been already dealt with by others better qualified. The arguments of A. H. Finn and James Orr, repeated and expanded in recent commentaries by E. J. Young, O. T. Allis, D. Kidner, R. K. Harrison and H. Leupold, convincingly demonstrate that Moses was the compiler of Genesis. These books have never been refuted but are largely ignored, one fears, in the Teacher Training Colleges of Britain. Perhaps these pages may help some to see that the tremendous *truths* of

Genesis 1–11 could have come only by Divine revelation to great men of God (Adam, Noah, Shem etc.) rather than from myth-spinning novelists of Iron-Age Israel.

A final word to those who may disagree with the author's conclusions. It is generally allowed that Religious Education today should be non-doctrinaire and open-ended. I suggest this means that in any discussion of Genesis 1–11 *both* points of view should be mentioned—Creation and Evolution—as mutually exclusive theories believed by different groups of intelligent and educated people. To write off creationists as 'blind fundamentalists', or to give children the impression that '*all* scientists believe in evolution', is to betray our own ignorance of one of the most powerful intellectual movements in 'Tomorrow's World'.

GENESIS CHAPTER ONE

Panorama of Creation — Mythical 'millions-of-years' — Miracle of instant Day/Night — Mythical 'creation-hymn.' — Miracle of atmosphere — Mythical 'Hebrew-idea-of-the-universe' — Miracle of symbiosis — Mythical origin of life from non-life — Miracle of God's clocks — Mythical origin of the solar system — Miracles of sea-creatures — Myths of their evolution — Miracles of flight — Archaepoteryx a link? — Miracles of instinct — Mythical horse-tale — Man a miracle, man-ape a myth — Miracle of perfection — Myth of Darwinism — Change and chance — Mathematics and probability.

DAY ONE

Verse 1.   In the beginning God created the heaven and the earth.

Note 1—Every river has its source and every story has a beginning.

These words teach us that the Universe had a *definite beginning in time.* It has not existed from all eternity, as ancient Greek philosphers believed.

Q.—What was God doing before He created heaven and earth?

Answer—We don't know, and it doesn't matter. (see Deuteronomy 29.29)
    All we need to know about God—
        what He has done and what He plans to do—
    is written in the 66 books from Genesis to Revelation.

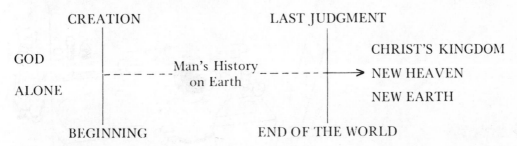

Q. – Who made God?

Answer—God is the Maker of all things, so nobody made Him.
    The Bible never tries to prove that God exists, because everyone knows by

instinct that Someone must have made this amazingly complex and wonder-filled world. (Romans 1.19—20)

Note 2—There are many signs that the universe is like a clock running down.

Therefore it must once have been wound up: e.g. the Sun loses weight at about 4 million tons a second.
It cannot have been doing this for ever.
So the Sun must have had a beginning.

Note 3—Probably this verse is a kind of heading to the whole chapter.

'Heaven' here means 'space'.
Sun, moon and stars were not created until the 4th Day (v.14).

Q.—How old is the Universe?

Answer—An illustration may help us to see the right answer.
One evening you come home from school and find the bath-tub half full of hot water—say 50°C. How long has the water been in the bath? There could be several theories:

a—the water came out of the tap nearly boiling and has cooled for a long time.

b—the water was run into the bath at 75°C and has been cooling for less than an hour.

c—the water has been in the bath only 5 minutes because your Mother knew what time you would come from school and made it just the right temperature.

Which theory is right?

You could never prove any one of them by mathematics.
The sensible answer is: Ask your Mother! —because she ran the water in.

The bath water puzzle.

In the same way scientists have many theories of how the Earth came to be just the right temperature for plants, animals and Man.

Some scientists believe that the Earth came out of the Sun ('boiling hot') and has been cooling for millions of years.

Other scientists believe that God made the Earth very much as we find it today (we shall see later what changes have taken place).

Scientifically it is impossible to PROVE which theory is right because nobody was there to observe what happened. So the sensible answer to the question 'How old is the Universe?' is:

Ask God! —because He made it.

That means, study the Bible.

In Genesis (the Greek word for 'beginning') He has given us an exact chronology (system of dating), and we shall discuss it in chapter 5.

For the time being, think about this:

1—Dr. Henry Morris, an engineer who has spent 30 years studying modern methods of dating, in his 'Scientific Creationism' (1974)[16] writes: 'Contrary to popular opinion, the actual *facts* of science correlate (agree) better with a young age for the earth than with the old evolutionary belief . . . 10,000 years seems to be the outside limit'.

2—Dr. David B. Gower, D.Sc., Ph.D., F.R.I.C., Reader in Biochemistry at Guy's Hospital, London, comes to much the same conclusion in his 'Radiometric Dating Methods' (1975).[61]

Note 4—We now know that the earth is held in 'position' in space by gravity pull from the sun. But of course the God who made the solar system and the 'law' of gravity is not subject to His own laws. HE could sustain the earth in mid-space as easily without gravity as with it.

Note 5—The earth was created *first*—before sun-moon-and-stars—to show its supreme importance, from God's point of view.

We shall discuss this again in the Notes on vv.14—18.

Verse 2.   And the earth was formless and void (*or* a waste and emptiness), and darkness was over the surface of the deep;
and the Spirit of God was moving (*or* hovering) over the surface of the waters.

(The translation used in this book is the New American Standard Bible, 1973. It is more accurate than the Revised Standard Version).

Note 1—The words 'formless and void' are used in Jeremiah 4.23 to describe a country desolate and uninhabited. So here they emphasise that the earth was lifeless and unfit for habitation until God transformed it into a world full of life and beauty.

Eagle hovering.

Note 2—The whole surface was covered with (probably salt) WATER. Some scientists think they have discovered the age of the oceans by dividing the amount of salt that goes into them every year (from rivers) into the total mass of water (300 million cubic miles).

But there is no reason at all why God could not have put the salt into the water from the very beginning.[39]

Verses 2 and 3

Note 3—It is very hard for a land-lubber to imagine a shoreless ocean as described here. Only by God's revelation could Moses (or Adam) have known that all the continents were submerged, once-upon-a-time.

Note 4—The word 'was moving' is used in Deuteronomy 32.11 of an eagle hovering over her eaglets, waiting to see them start flying.

So the Spirit of God was watching over the vast shoreless ocean, waiting for the appearance of Light and Life.

Verse 3   And God said, 'Let there be light!' —and there was light.

Note 1—Since the sun was not created until Day 4, this light cannot have been the sun's light.

Perhaps God did things this way to show that HE—not the sun—is the source of all light and all life (see v.11).

Note 2—Many other ancient peoples (Babylonians, Egyptians, Chinese, Greeks etc.) had 'creation stories', but *only* the Hebrews believed that light came before the sun.

This proves that the author of Genesis was an *original* writer and did *not* copy the myths and legends of surrounding nations, as some textbooks say.

Note 3—God's *method* of creation is here shown to be
   a)   out of nothing
   b)   in no time
   c)   instant perfection, with no 'experiments'
   d)   simply by 'ordering' it.

Contrast man's method, e.g. Thomas Edison conducted thousands of experiments for two years, using many different kinds of material, before he succeeded in producing an electric light bulb on October 19th, 1879. Even then it burned out in less than two days!

Edison's electric lamp 1879.

Note 4—God said = God wished it to happen
   and did what He wanted done.
Throughout the Bible God is spoken of as a real *person*,
   as a King giving orders,
   as a master-workman fulfilling His own designs (Proverbs 8.27—30).

Verse 4.   **And God saw that the light was good;**
                 and God separated the light from the darkness.

Verse 5a.   **And God called the light Day**
                 and the darkness He called Night.

Note 1—This is an extra-ordinarily interesting verse because it clearly implies that light and darkness, Night and Day, are *both present at the same time* on the surface of the earth, since the separation took place before the first evening.

   For thousands of years Man has been familiar with the line dividing light from darkness on the face of the *moon*, but until Copernicus (A.D.1543) no one had any idea that (to an observer in Space) a similar line divides light from darkness on the face of the *earth*. In fact it is only in the last 15 years, since astronauts began to take photographs of the earth from 'way out', that we have become familiar with the idea of our globe being partly light and partly dark. Neither Moses nor anyone else B.C. could possibly have had such a picture in mind. Only God had; and He gave the author a 'God's-eye-view'.

Light and darkness of the spinning earth.

Note 2—Exactly what the light-source was, nobody can tell. We only know it must have been localised—like the sun—in one spot. If it had been all round the earth at once, there could have been no separation of light from darkness, nor 'evening' and 'morning'.

Verse 5b.   And there was evening and morning, one day.

Note 1—Much argument has centred around the meaning of the word Day in Genesis One. In 5a it means *daylight,* obviously, and in 5b it means 24 hours.

This double usage is the same in Hebrew, Greek and English.
We say e.g. 'Tigers hunt at night and sleep during the day' (= daylight) but also 'Half a million babies are born every day' (= 24 hours).

Q.—How could there be a 'day' before the sun existed?

Answer—Easily, because the length of a day depends *not* on the sun but *on the earth's rotation on its own axis.*

Once again the Bible was scientifically correct, 3000 years before Copernicus.

The 'Creation-Hymn' Myth

Before going on we shall dispose of a popular idea that these verses are a sort of (non-scientific) hymn, with Days 1, 2 and 3 parallel to Days 4, 5 and 6.

What does the Bible actually say?

Day 1. Creation of Earth, Ocean, Light	Day 4. Sun, moon, stars
2. Air, clouds	5. Sea-creatures, birds
3. Dry land, vegetation	6. Land animals, Man

From this you can see that the only 'parallel' days are 3 and 6. To make 1 parallel to 4 and 2 to 5, we would have to move the Sea-creatures up from Day 5 to Day 4.

Conclusion—the hymn idea is another 19th century myth.

Note 3—The word 'evening' implies a gradual approach of darkness *after* light, so it cannot mean the total darkness of verse 2.
Therefore it must mean the evening which came on *after* the creation of light.

Experiment

1. Set a globe in a pitch-dark room.
2. Shine a torch directly on it, i.e. at right-angles.
3. Mark with a pin the spot (on the globe) which is nearest to the torch.
4. Call this point P.
5. Now rotate the globe to the right (i.e. eastward).
6. Your point P will pass into shadow when it has rotated 90° which is equivalent to 6 hours, of which the last hour might be called 'evening'.
7. Continue to rotate the globe through a further 180°.
8. As point P moves out of darkness back into the light, 'morning' has come.

Q.—But how is this 'one day'? P has moved only through 270° = 18 hours.

Answer—a—It is reasonable to suppose that the water-covered globe had been in existence for 6 hours before God created light.

b—Also, it had been rotating throughout those 6 hours.

c—So, at the moment of the earth's creation, point P was exactly at the point where morning would dawn 24 hours later.

d—So, for point P the first Day consisted of:

> 6 hours total darkness
> + 6 hours light (ending with 'evening')
> + 12 hours night (ending with 'morning')

TOTAL 24 hours

9. So the first Day was really 18 hours darkness + 6 hours light.
10. Day 2 was the first 'normal' day. (see Diagram).

Special Note. Some Bible teachers may feel that it is a waste of time to go into such details. Other teachers may feel that it is a waste of time to go into the geographical detail of 300 place-names in Acts. But just as faith is strengthened by discovering that every place mentioned by Luke is a *real* place on a *real* map, and that St. Paul's journeys perfectly accord with *real history*—so, I believe, faith is strengthened by study which reveals that the words of Genesis have real meaning in terms of real physics and real geography, and are perfectly in accord with *real science.*

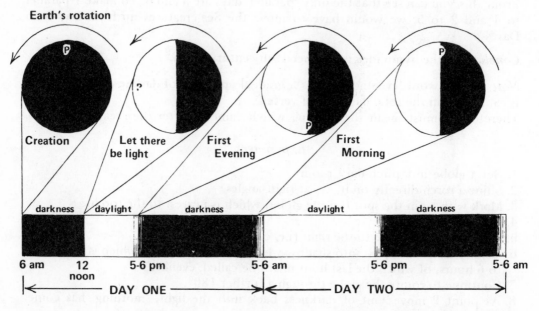

Experimental diagram (first two days of Creation)

'You will see a picture like this . . .'

DAY TWO

Verse 6. And God said, 'Let there be an expanse in the midst of the waters, and let it separate the waters from the waters'.

Note 1—The Hebrew word for 'expanse' here denotes the AIR or ATMOSPHERE.

The RSV translation 'firmament' (implying something hard and solid) is a *mis*-translation based on a mistake made by those who put the Hebrew Bible into Greek around 250 B.C. (see Notes on v.7).

Note 2—In no other creation-stories do we find such importance given to the air/atmosphere. Once again, only Genesis is scientifically correct.

So far from being 'nothing', air is essential to all life on land.

Why do astronauts need oxygen on the Moon?

Because there is no AIR, and God never intended people to live there.

Verse 7. And God made the expanse, and separated the waters which were under the expanse from the waters which were above the expanse;

Note 1—This verse has often been misunderstood. In some RE books you will see a picture like the one above which is supposed to show that the Hebrews thought the blue sky was a solid glass dome or metal plate having windows, and when these 'windows' were opened the 'waters above the firmament' poured down onto the earth.

Note 2—This picture is a real MYTH. *No such idea exists in the Bible,* which says that 'God binds up the waters in His thick clouds' (Job 26.8). 'Windows of heaven' is used not only about rain but also of God giving *grain* (II Kings 7.19). Birds are often called 'fowls of heaven' and are said to fly 'in the heaven' (Deut. 4.17; Jer.8.7). If heaven were a solid plate, obviously birds could not fly in it.

Note 3—The simplest explanation of 'waters above the expanse' seems to be—clouds. They can truly be said to be 'above' the sky/atmosphere and yet at the same time 'in' the sky/atmosphere; just as a submarine is by definition an 'under-sea-boat' (German 'unterseeboot') yet at the same time 'in' the sea.

Note 4—However, many scientists believe that there is a deeper meaning in this verse: before the Flood there was a water 'canopy' all round the earth, trapping the sun's rays more effectively than our present atmosphere does, and giving a semi-tropical climate to every part of the world (see diagram)[1].
So 'waters above the expanse' would include both clouds and 'canopy'.

Note 5—In Job 37.16 God asks this question:
'Do you know the balancings of the clouds?
—the wondrous works of Him who is perfect in knowledge?'
Certainly this 'balancing' is one of the marvels of creation. Man has never made anything to equal it; and man is still unable accurately to predict the weather more than a few days in advance.

Note 6—Another interesting verse in Job is 28.25:
'God imparted weight to the wind.'
No one realized that the air has weight until Evangelista Torricelli, a pupil of Galileo, constructed the first barometer in 1643.
But it was written in the Bible three thousand years before that!

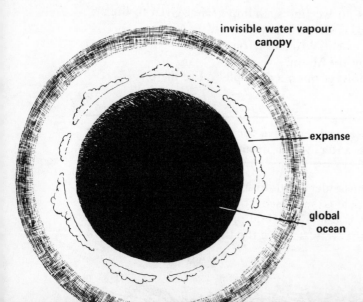

invisible water vapour
canopy

expanse

global
ocean

Earth's atmosphere before the Flood

Thunder cloud

Note 7—Though Genesis was written in the Near East, where the annual rainfall is only a few inches, the description of clouds as 'waters' is strictly accurate from the point of view of world-science. It has been computed that there are 45,000 thunderstorms *daily* somewhere in the world, and each thundercloud carries about 100,000 tons of water. (WBE)

Verse 8.   And God called the expanse Heaven.
And there was evening and there was morning, a second day.

The separation of the sea and the dry land

DAY THREE

Verse 9.   And God said, 'Let the waters under the heaven be gathered together unto one place, and let the dry land appear': and it was so.

Note 1—It is probable that the highest mountains were not 'pushed up' until after the Flood, and the deep ocean basins were hollowed out at the same time to hold the vast quantities of surplus water (Psalm 104.6–9).

So the pre-Flood world was flatter than ours (though still round, of course!) and the seas shallower. 'Unto one place' = inter-connected oceans at the same mean-sea-level, and seems to imply that there were then no inland seas like e.g. the Aral Sea (160 ft. above m.s.l.) or the Dead Sea (1300 ft. below m.s.l.).

Note 2—Some scientists find it hard to believe that the continents could have been raised up in one day from below the 'deep' sea.

But nobody really knows what caused land first to appear, and God's power in creation cannot be limited.

Even now the strength of subterranean (underground) forces is terrific. When the island of Krakatoa exploded (27 August 1883), five cubic miles of rock and earth were blown up to a height of 90,000 feet.

Krakatoa explodes

The barren moon

Verse 10.   And God called the dry land Earth; and the gathering together of the waters He called Seas: and God saw that it was good.

Note 1—Why did God name these five things—Day, Night, Atmosphere, Earth, Sea? (notice the restricted meaning here of 'earth'. In Hebrew as in English the word can mean *both* the whole globe *and* the stuff you dig up in the garden).

Answer—perhaps a) to call attention to their importance
              b) to show His unique power over them.

God did not name the trees or fruits or fish, birds and animals. That was left to man; because Man has the power to cultivate and organise plant life, and to tame, breed or kill animals.

But man has *no* power to change the Day-Night sequence,
              no power to control the Weather, Earth or Sea.

Earthquakes, volcanoes, tides and storms remind us that GOD alone is Lord of these.

Note 2—Also it is interesting to note that *none of these five things exist on the Moon:* no atmosphere, no sea, and no fertile land.

The Moon has sunlight for 14 earth-days every month, and 14 days darkness. Temperatures vary from 260° F to −280° F. If we had the same, all life on earth would be scorched or frozen to death.

But God put the earth spinning at just the right speed to produce just the right length of day and night and just the right temperature for every living thing.

Note 3—Jeremiah 5.22 throws more light on this verse. God says:

'Will you not fear Me? I have placed the sand as a boundary to the sea, an eternal law, nor will the sea pass over it.'

This is scientifically correct. Sand is a very remarkable substance—practically indestructible, everlasting. Rocks can be torn apart or eroded by the sea; earth can be dissolved and disintegrated; but sand defies the fiercest storms.

Verse 11.   And God said, 'Let the earth sprout vegetation, plants yielding seed, and fruit trees bearing fruit after their kind, with seed in them, on the earth'; and it was so.

Creation of plants

Verses 10 and 11

Figs and fig wasp

FIRST LIFE ON EARTH

Note 1—The Theory of Evolution (we shall call it T.O.E. from now on) says: life first 'evolved' in the ocean, and millions of years later spread to the land. The 'evidence' for this is marine fossils discovered in the lowest water-laid rocks (called 'Cambrian').

Note 2—However, if most of these fossils are the remains of creatures destroyed by Noah's Flood, as many scientists believe, it would be perfectly natural to find shellfish at the bottom because shellfish have always lived at the lowest levels of life, hundreds of feet below land plants and fruit trees.

Note 3—It is also significant that fossil pollen of pine trees has been found at the bottom of the Grand Canyon, Arizona. This proves that *pine trees existed at the same time as the earliest kinds of marine life.* (See 'The Grand Canyon Story' by Clifford Burdick, Bible-Science Newsletter April 1968. Dr. Burdick is a professional geologist).[3]

Note 4—Here for the first time we find the phrase 'after their kind', which is repeated 8 times in the chapter. This again flatly contradicts TOE which states that *all* kinds of life evolved from *one* kind of living thing in the pea-soup ocean of long ago. But evolutionists cannot show even one kind of tree changing into another kind of tree. You can cross an orange with a lemon and produce (no, not a grapefruit) an 'oramon', but it is still the same *kind* of fruit, i.e. citrus.

Similarly there are hundreds of varieties of grape, and stories of wines and vines go back thousands of years, but grapes are still grapes and never look like turning into plums.

Note 5—Many trees and plants depend on insects for pollination; in some cases the insect in turn depends on the plant for its larva's food. Two examples are specially interesting:

a—In Mexico there are about 30 species of 'yucca' plant. The yucca can be pollinated only by a yucca-moth, 'the various species of which are *each adapted to a separate species of the yucca*' (EB). Without the yucca-moth the yucca plant will bear no seeds: without (a few) yucca-seeds to eat the yucca-moth larva cannot survive!

b—The Moreton Bay fig of Australia and the Smyrna fig of Turkey both depend on wasps for pollination. Attempts to grow these fruit in Hawaii and California completely failed until the right wasp from the right country was introduced. [17]

According to TOE these insects just 'happened' to evolve at the right time in the right place for the right plant; but mathematicians tell us that the chances of such events 'happening' are about infinity to one, or zero probability.

Note 6—In 1864 Louis Pasteur proved conclusively that life comes only from life. Non-living material can never produce living things. Every time a surgeon does an operation he relies on this universal truth, that no bacteria can reach a wound so long as his instruments are 'sterile'.

In spite of this some scientists are trying to make out that millions of years ago things were different, so life might have come from non-life by a fluke in 500 million B.C. But by this sort of reasoning anything 'might have happened'. A cat might have had puppies, or a baby might have popped out of a dinosaur's egg.

Real science is limited to what has been *observed* by humans. So real science can tell us nothing positive about origins: it can tell us only that *we know nothing*. Therefore we should admit our ignorance and turn to God's revelation. As one wise man has written:

'In the first page of the Bible a child may learn more in one hour than all the scientists of the world learned without it in thousands of years.'

Let us pause a moment to consider the wonder of plant life.

FLOWERS. There are about 200,000 kinds living today. The largest is the giant Rafflesia of Indonesia, up to 3 foot across and weighing 15 pounds. Smallest is the duckweed, 1/50 of an inch long and 1/63 of an inch wide.

Anything 'might have' happened!

There are mountain flowers, prairie flowers, desert flowers, beach flowers, meadow flowers, swamp flowers; parasitic flowers and carnivorous flowers. Even in one family, the Rose, there are thousands of varieties. Their beauty and fragrance have been famous since the dawn of civilisation.

TREES. There are about 20,000 kinds.

They include the oldest living things on earth, California bristlecone pines (4000–5000 years, probably going back to Noah's Flood), and the largest— sequoias, with trunks up to 36 feet wide.

The largest seeds in the world belong to the coco-de-mer of the Seychelles Islands. One nut may weigh up to 50 pounds.

Trees have a thousand-and-one uses for mankind and animals—for food and fuel, for shelter, shade, and ships, for art and ornament. There is even a Traveller's Tree in Madagascar (Malagasy) which stores a pint of water in the base of each of its long leaf-stalks! (WBE)

FRUIT. What a marvellous variety we enjoy every year—enough to suit all tastes and supply most of the vitamins and minerals which our bodies need. In our own little island there are apples, pears, grapes, cherries, redcurrants, white-currants, blackcurrants, gooseberries, strawberries, raspberries, blackberries, loganberries, mulberries, plums—any more?

From Europe come oranges and lemons, tangerines, apricots, peaches, nectarines. Going further afield we find dates, olives, figs, limes, fifty varieties of mango, papaya, guava, banana, grapefruit, jackfruit, breadfruit, passionfruit, pineapple, custard-apple, lychees and mangosteen. If Adam had only these to choose from (and he may have had many more), he certainly had no excuse for wanting the Forbidden Fruit as well.

DAY FOUR

Verse 14.   And God said, 'Let there be lights in the expanse of heaven, to divide the day from the night;
and let them be for signs and for seasons, and for days and years;

Verse 15.   And let them be for lights in the expanse of heaven to give light upon the earth: and it was so.

Note 1—Here we meet a problem. If the sun moon and stars were set *in* the expanse (RV 'Firmament') of heaven, does that not prove that the Hebrews thought the sky was solid?

Answer—No: here the language of Scripture is 'phenomenal', i.e. describing how the sun etc. *appeared.* We say, 'I can see the 'plane *in* my binoculars' when we really mean *through* my binoculars.

Similarly the stars appeared to be in the sky but were really beyond it and seen *through* the atmosphere.

Sir Isaac Newton

Note 2—Many scientists believe that the sun existed before the earth, but no scientist can prove it. The idea that the 9 planets 'spun off' the sun millions of years ago, raises as many problems as it pretends to solve.

For example, six of the nine planets have satellites of their own (like our Moon)—32 satellites in all. Of these 32, eleven are orbiting their 'mother' planets *in the wrong direction,* that is to say in the opposite direction to the mother's rotation.

Sir Isaac Newton, who was the first to discover how the solar system hangs together, believed that God made it very much as it now is. No new facts have been brought to light to show that Newton was wrong.

Note 3—Why did God create the sun moon and stars (which includes 'fixed' stars, planets, comets and meteors)?

The obvious answer may not be the right answer.

We think of the sun as essential for life, but God made every kind of plant life before the sun appeared. No doubt He could also have made the animals able to survive without the aid of any particular star.

These verses show that God's main purpose in creating the sun moon and stars was for

MEASUREMENT AND DIVISIONS OF TIME

From the very beginning God wanted man to be a chronologer (time-measurer), so that we might live orderly lives. Archaeology, the study of ancient civilizations, indicates that Early Man understood this purpose very well and tried to fulfil it. In Genesis 5 and 11 we shall see how Abraham's ancestors successfully kept family records over hundreds and even thousands of years.

a.   *Day and Night.* Obviously the day is meant for work, normally, and the night for rest and sleep. But some people (e.g. sailors) have to keep awake at night, and in hot countries the cool hours of darkness are best for travelling. So the gentle light of the moon, too, is useful. The Bible calls the moon 'the faithful witness' (Psalm 89.37), perhaps because it simply reflects the light of the sun. (The astronauts who landed there discovered that the moon's surface is covered with a glassy-sand substance which is ideal for reflecting).

b.   The *Phases of the Moon* have been used as week-measurements for thousands of years. 'Primitive' man was a lot cleverer than most of us today; by looking at the moon he could tell exactly how far the month (29 days) had progressed.

Verses 14 and 15

Phases of the moon

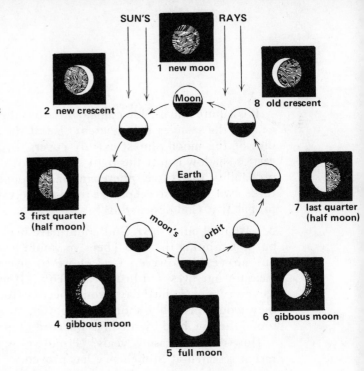

SUN'S   RAYS

1 new moon

8 old crescent

2 new crescent

Moon

Earth

moon's   orbit

3 first quarter
(half moon)

7 last quarter
(half moon)

4 gibbous moon

6 gibbous moon

5 full moon

Moon-landings are a magnificent achievement, but ten minutes study of the Bible will tell us more than a hundred Apollo-s *why* the moon is where it is.

(Incidentally, before Apollo 11 landed, scientists predicted that there would be dust scores of feet thick on the moon's surface—since it was supposed to be 4000 million years old. It was a big shock when the astronauts found only an inch or two—another pointer to the *young* age of our Universe).

c.   *Eclipses* of the sun and moon have been used for at least 4000 years to measure time. The Babylonians, Egyptians and Greeks knew that a solar eclipse takes place at intervals of 18 years and 11 days, and could make correct predictions. This has enabled modern historians to check dates in ancient history with perfect accuracy, e.g.

'The most famous of ancient eclipses was a total eclipse of the sun on 28 May 585 B.C. during a battle between the Lydians and the Medes. The portent (= sign) induced them to make peace' (EB): A man named Thales had predicted this eclipse from the previous one which occurred on 18 May 603 B.C.

Q.—How do eclipses happen?

Answer—1) when the moon comes exactly between the earth and the sun
2) when earth's shadow passes over the moon (see diagram)

SUN

MOON

Eclipse of the sun

Eclipse of the moon

SUN

MOON

EARTH

It is a quite remarkable coincidence that the *apparent* size of the moon is almost exactly the same as the *apparent* size of the sun, viewed from our planet. So the disc of the moon almost exactly covers the sun during a solar eclipse. Similarly earth's shadow is just the right size to blot out the moon for a lunar eclipse. The probability that three spheres in space should *by chance* so interact as to produce these two types of eclipse at regular intervals, is about one to infinity, or zero probability. God designed it!

d.   What about *years?* God could have made the earth rotating on its own axis but not orbiting the sun. Then we would have had day/night and moon-months, but no years. However, God chose to give us a longer time-span by which to measure our lives and historical events. (If everyone in your family had a birthday every *month,* birthdays would become too common and too much trouble; so they would probably soon be forgotten altogether!) So He set the earth rolling round the sun, held by the invisible cord of gravity.

How do we measure years? 'Primitive' man was an excellent astronomer, as recent research at Stonehenge has proved.   He measured a year by the *solstices*

Stonehenge

('sun standing still') which occur twice annually. In summer the sun appears to rise and set farther *north* every day until June 21st, when it goes into reverse and begins to rise and set farther *south* every day. This continues until December 21st, when once again it changes and starts to move north. (While changing direction the sun appears to 'stand still': hence the word 'solstice', from the Latin.) This is known as a Solar Year: 365 days, 5 hours 48 minutes 46 seconds.

Ancient Britons' calendar 'was a highly developed arrangement involving an exact knowledge of the length of the year . . . they set up many stations for observing the 18-year cycle' of the moon. This quotation comes from a book called 'Megalithic (= Big Stone) Sites in Britain' by Professor A. Thom of Oxford University. He has spent 30 years studying hundreds of monuments like Stonehenge.

The second method of measuring a year is *by the stars.* Their position changes slightly every night, until after 365 days 6 hours 9 minutes and 9.6 seconds they are in exactly the same position as they were before. This method too was well

Navigation

known to ancient civilizations. The Egyptians measured their year by the rising of Sirius, the brightest star, over the Nile at dawn. We call this a Sidereal (= star) Year and our most accurate clocks—atomic chronometers— are adjusted by reference to it.

e. Obviously *hours* (a man-made division) can be told by means of a sun-dial. Also, anyone who really knows astronomy can tell the time at night by the stars; and Professor Thom believes the ancient Britons could do this too.[40]

f. *Navigation.* Most people know the North Star and the two 'pointers' in the Plough constellation. Aeroplane pilots still use these and other stars for navigation, as sailors have done for thousands of years. With the help of a sextant and an almanac you can find exactly where you are on the earth or sea or in the sky—if you can see the stars. This is probably what the Bible means by 'SIGNS': pointers or direction-finders.

g. Another very useful method of measuring time is by the *Tides.* Our mighty oceans are always on the move. The pull of the moon's gravitation causes two high tides every day, but the moon's daily movement of 12 degrees round the earth makes the tide later by 48 minutes every day.

So people who live by the sea have another 'sign' by which to tell the time, even if they can't see the sun or moon. There are also neap (extra low) and spring (extra high) tides at regular intervals every month, according to the sun's position relative to the moon. (Incidentally it has been calculated that if the moon were only 10% nearer to us, tides would sweep right over the continents. God's infinite wisdom and power have put the Earth and Moon exactly the right distance apart).[41]

h. Another use of the stars was for telling *Seasons,* before farmers had printed calendars. A Greek poet writing about 750 B.C. says:

'Begin your harvest when the Pleiades are rising   (May)
and your ploughing when they are going to set.'   (November)
'Set your slaves to winnow the grain when strong Orion first appears.' (July)

Most of the world's population still live by farming, and many have no calendar except the one God has provided in the stars.

i. What about the *Planets?* why did God put these 'wandering' stars in the sky?
They cannot be said to mark seasons or years, but it seems they are useful as
a special sort of 'sign':

The Star in the East, which led the Wise Men to Bethlehem, was probably a
conjunction (joining together) of the planets Jupiter, Saturn and Mars, in B.C.
4 or 5. (The date of Jesus' birth was wrongly calculated by a monk named
Dionysius in 550 A.D. Herod the Great, who slaughtered the innocent babies of
Bethlehem, died in 'B.C.' 4, and obviously Jesus must have been born before
Herod's death.) The conjunction was no 'coincidence' but planned by God,
when He made the planets, to be a special SIGNAL announcing the arrival of
Jesus Christ, his Son.

Other Bible verses (e.g. Luke 21.25) speak of 'signs in sun and moon and
stars' as a warning of Christ's second coming to Earth. This may include another special conjunction of planets.

The planets are useful in another way too. Being so much nearer to us than
any star, they can be studied in much greater detail. From the planets we learn
how 'lucky' we are not to be roasting on Venus at 980° F, or freezing on Pluto
at −300° F;
and how improbable it is that life exists anywhere else in the Universe.
Genesis 1.14 strongly suggests that the planets were made for man,
not man for the planets.

The great comet of 1861

Meteor shower

j.   In bygone ages *Comets* (stars with 'tails') were often regarded as 'bad omens'. You may know the famous lines spoken by Calpurnia in 'Julius Caesar':
   'When beggars die, there are no comets seen:
   The heavens themselves blaze forth the death of princes.'
The Bible does not support this idea, but comets do remind us that the movements of heavenly bodies are partly regular and *partly unpredictable.*

   For example, Halley's Comet has been reappearing every 76½ years, roughly, for at least 2200 years, and we expect its return again in 1986. But also a new comet may appear any night and startle the astronomers.

   A million mysteries remain hidden even to our most powerful telescopes, because as the Bible says:
   'Lo, these are but the outskirts of His ways,
   And how small a whisper do we hear of Him.' (Job 26.14)
   Another interesting fact: comets are burning out at a terrific rate and cannot possibly be millions of years old—they would have burned out and disappeared long ago.[16]

   And since comets are part of the solar system, it seems probable that the age of our sun and planets too is to be measured only in thousands rather than millions of years.

k.   'Shooting stars' are really *Meteors,* which travel in varying orbits and velocities around the sun but cannot be seen till they hit our atmosphere, when they blaze brilliantly and burn out in a few seconds. Meteors that reach earth before burning up are called *meteorites.*

   At enormous expense, and after years of preparation, Man has been able to land two men and a small spacecraft on the Moon. But God, at the flick of an eyelid, so to speak, can fling hundred-ton meteorites onto our Earth. In 1908 the famous Tunguska meteorite hit Siberia, scorching a 20-mile area and flattening 80 million trees like matchsticks. People hundreds of miles away saw it in full daylight, and the blast was felt at a distance of 50 miles. (WBE)

   Such an event might well be called a *sign* or reminder, of that coming 'day of the Lord' when **'the heavens shall pass away with a great noise, and the elements shall be dissolved with intense heat, and the earth and everything in it shall be burned up'** (II Peter 3.10).

The Tunguska meteorite

(Another incidental fact: meteoric dust is falling from outer space at the rate of 14 million tons a year. If this has been going on for 4500 million years (the supposed age of Earth), there should be a layer of dust 182 feet thick all over the planet. But where is it? Neither here nor on the Moon. More evidence that both Earth and Moon are much 'younger' than some scientists would have us believe).[16]

Note 1—The Bible account of creation shows that *Astrology* ('what the stars foretell') is pure superstition and pseudo- (false) science.

Stars are lifeless *things* and can influence human affairs no more than sticks or stones. But from very early times man has been tempted to worship these mysterious, distant, beautiful orbs (see Job 31.26–7).

The only true message of the stars was put into verse by Joseph Addison in 1700 A.D.: They are

'forever singing as they shine:
"The hand that made us is Divine"'!'

Verse 16. And God made the two great lights,
    the greater light to govern the day
    and the lesser light to govern the night:
    (He made) the stars also.

Verse 17. And God set them in the expanse of heaven to give light on the earth,

Verse 18. and to govern the day and the night, and to separate the light from the darkness: and God saw that it was good.

Verses 14, 15, 16, 17 and 18

Note 1—v.16 does not mean, of course, that the sun is the biggest star in the universe—only that it gives *us* more light.

Note 2—This 'governing' of the day and night is not so obvious to modern city-dwellers, but it is still a fact. Some birds and animals are definitely 'day' creatures, while others instinctively choose night-hunting (badgers, hedgehogs), night-flying (owls, bats), and night-singing (nightingales). Day-birds like rooks fly back to their nests in the evening: night-birds return home before dawn. They are *governed* by the sun and moon.

Note 3—Once again we see the vital importance of TIME in the life of Man. God could have implanted an automatic (instinctive) clock in the head of every human. But instead of this He set the world spinning and made a fixed point in space (the sun) by reference to which we can organise our lives.

If it were not for this 'governing' it would be impossible to plan a school time-table (9.0 a.m. would mean *nothing*) or celebrate Christmas Day, because there would be no calendar.

Note 4—The *Perfection* of God's arrangement is seen also in

a. our distance from the sun—exactly right for temperature.
If the average temperature of the earth were raised only two or three degrees, the ice sheets and glaciers would melt,
and London and New York would be 200 feet under water.

b. the size of the earth. If it were only 10% larger or smaller, life as we know it could not exist on this planet.

c. the 23½° tilt of earth's axis. If the sun were always over the equator, with no change of seasons, the proportion of earth's surface fit for cultivation and habitation would be reduced by half.[41]

d. a layer of ozone (a special kind of oxygen) 40 miles above the earth, protecting us from the sun's killer rays.

Note 5—Before leaving the subject of astronomy we should note two more remarkable verses in the Bible:

a. **'He (God) hangs the earth upon nothing'** (Job 26.7).
This scientific truth was unknown to ancient astronomers before 300 B.C., but God revealed it to Job at least 1000 years before that. Contrast with this the ancient oriental idea that the world rests on the back of an elephant standing on a tortoise!

The sun's killer rays

'He hangs the earth upon nothing'
(p.25, Note 5a)

Creation of sea creatures and birds

b. **'The host of heaven (i.e. stars) cannot be counted, and the sand of the sea cannot be measured'** (Jeremiah 33.22).

In the days of Jeremiah (600 B.C.) stars could be seen only with the naked eye—not more than 3000 of them on a clear night.

22 centuries later Galileo with his telescope caught a glimpse of the vastly greater number away out in space.

But it was not till this century that Sir James Jeans (1930) wrote: 'The total number of stars is roughly equal to the total number of grains of sand on all the sea-shores of all the world'.[38] So this scientific truth was revealed by God in the Bible 2500 years before it was discovered by man.

Verse 19.   And there was evening and there was morning, a fourth day.

Note 1—This verse shows that the 4th day was the same time-span as the first three, i.e. 24 hours.

At some point the light of v.3 must have merged or perhaps condensed into the sun: so Genesis is now speaking in terms of *solar* days.

Note 2—Popular science often tells us that 'our Earth is *no longer* the centre of the universe. There may be other inhabited planets and they may be more highly developed than ours'.

This is too big a subject for discussion here, but it is worth noting that

a.   There is no scientific *evidence* that life exists anywhere else in space. ('Chariots of the Gods' shows only that ancient Man had a highly developed technology. With this the Bible fully agrees.)

b.   If there were other inhabited planets, this would not contradict anything written in the Bible.

    c.   Importance is not measured by physical centrality.
London is not the geographical centre of Britain,
and Rome was not the centre of the Roman Empire.

    d.   The importance of planet Earth is proved by the fact that the Son of God was born on it and gave His life for Earth-ians.

Note 3—The question of light-years, age of the stars etc. is dealt with in the author's 'GREAT BRAIN ROBBERY' ch.3 and Appendix A.

    The short answer is: Adam's *apparent* age was (say) 25 years, only one second after he was created.
In the same way the stars were created with a built-in *apparent* age which was much greater than their actual age.

    (For a fuller discussion of this point please see the review of 'GREAT BRAIN ROBBERY' by Dr. Boyd in the magazine 'SPECTRUM', September 1975, and the answer given by Dr. D. B. Gower and Dr. D. C. Watts).

Note 4—Professor J. C. Whitcomb in his book 'THE ORIGIN OF THE SOLAR SYSTEM' (1971) examines the many theories of how the earth and sun are supposed to have 'evolved'. He shows that every theory at some point fails to fit the facts. There is no *fact* of science which contradicts the Genesis statement that God made the earth first, and the sun-moon-and-stars later.[5]

DAY FIVE

Verse 20.   Then God said, 'Let the waters teem with swarms of living creatures, and let birds fly above the earth in the open expanse of the heavens.'

Verse 21.   And God created the great sea-monsters, and every living creature that moves, with which the waters swarmed after their kind, and every winged bird after its kind; and God saw that it was good.

Note 1—Evolutionists teach that the first animal life in the sea was something like an amoeba—so small that you need a microscope to see it. Of course even an amoeba is a very complicated creature, which only God could create. But the Bible says He made the BIGGEST creatures first.

Note 2—The largest whales weigh 150 tons (more than any dinosaur)—and (as you know) are mammals. Some scientists say the whale's ancestors once lived on land, but not a single fossil has ever been discovered of any creature half-way between a land-mammal and a sea-mammal.

    All sea-mammals (whales, seals, walruses, dolphins, dugong, sea-elephants etc.) are highly 'specialised'—very different from each other, yet each species perfectly adapted to its own particular kind of sea-life. For example the whale's ear and eye

Giant squid, whale shark and blue whale — comparative sizes of the largest known sea creatures.

are quite different from a land-mammal's, and mother-whale has an ingenious device for giving milk to her baby. The baby's snout fits snugly into his mother's body so that sea-water cannot get mixed with the milk, and his windpipe is prolonged above the gullet so that the milk cannot flow into his lungs. Such a device must have been perfect from the beginning—*both* in the mother *and* in the baby—for it to work at all. It could never have 'evolved' by gradual changes.[3]

Note 3—The bones in a whale's hip-muscles are said to be the remnants of 'hind-legs' which 'disappeared' when the whale became a swimmer instead of a walker. But these bones are found in only a few kinds of whale, out of a total of nearly 200 different species, so the 'hind-leg' explanation does not seem very satisfactory.[39]

Note 4—The enormous variety of marine life may be judged from these figures:

species of living mollusc (shell-fish)	100,000
species of fossil/extinct mollusc	100,000
species of crustacea (crabs, lobsters etc.)	30,000
species of vertebrate (backboned) fish	21,000

Molluscs range in size from snails as small as a grain of sand——to the giant squid 60 ft long;
from clams weighing half an ounce
   to the 500-pound Australian clam which can drown a diver.
Crabs can be as small as the pea-crab which lives inside mussels—
   or as big as the Japanese spider-crab, five foot across.
The smallest fish is the pygmy goby of the Philippines, less than half an inch long.
The largest is the whale shark, weighing up to 15 tons—
   twice as much as an African elephant. (WBE)

Verses 20 and 21

Some scientists say that all these vastly different creatures have evolved from the same 'protozoa' (tiny one-celled animals). But in the Cambrian (oldest fossil-bearing) rocks we find vertebrate fish and molluscs and crustacea *fully formed* with bones and shells. This fact confirms the Bible account of instantaneous creation of innumerable kinds of sea-creatures, all together.

Note 5—Intensive breeding experiments over the past 100 years have completely failed to show how any one kind of fish could ever change into another.

Note 6—Recently a mollusc called 'neopilina galathea' was dredged up from 11,700 feet below sea-level. It was supposed to have become extinct 280 million years ago, but there it was alive and well in 1957 A.D.![16]

The coelacanth tells the same story—supposed to be a 'primitive' fish that died out 60 million years ago, but several live ones have been caught in the Indian Ocean since 1938. Thus it seems most probable that fish have never changed from 'primitive' to 'modern', but have remained much the same since their creation.

Note 7—The dodo is now extinct, and the ostrich has survived; but this does not prove that the dodo was ancestor to the ostrich. They both lived together (i.e. at the same time)—500 years ago. So 'armoured' fish are now extinct, and the cod has survived; but this does not prove that the cod's ancestors were armoured.

Probably both kinds of fish lived together 5000 years ago (i.e. before the Flood).

Note 8—TOE is quite unable to explain hundreds of 'freaks' such as the electric eel, which catches its food by radar and can emit 300 volt shocks continuously—[43]

the sea-horse (the male broods the 200 eggs in his pouch)—

The robber-crab, which climbs coconut trees with its big set of claws, hammers a hole through the coconut 'eye',

then scoops out the coconut meat with a *small* set of claws specially designed for the purpose!—[48]

the dolphin's sonar, and friendliness to man—

the exquisite beauty, strength and symmetry of hundreds of sea-shells (some have a right-hand thread, some a left-hand thread—WHY??)—

the grunion of California beaches, a fish that lays its eggs on *land* at high-tide on a full-moon night, so that they get exactly the right interval of two weeks to incubate in the sand before the next extra-high tide pops the eggs open and washes the young fry out to sea.[42]

(WHO taught the grunion to time the tides?)—

Coelacanth

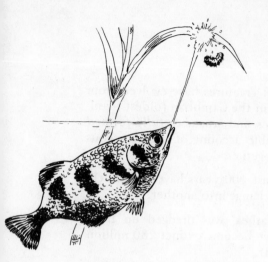

Archer fish

the archer-fish, aiming from below the water-surface, can shoot down an insect sitting on a twig *above* the surface. This means that the fish automatically allows for the refraction (bending) of light in water!

Verse 22.   **And God blessed them, saying, 'Be fruitful and multiply,**
and fill the waters in the seas,
and let birds multiply in the earth.'

Verse 23.   **And there was evening and there was morning, a fifth day.**

Note 1—'Which came first, the chicken or the egg?'
Here we find the true answer to an age-old question.
Birds were created full-grown, and immediately commanded to multiply. (God 'speaking' to fish etc. probably means that He put within them the *instinct* to do what He wanted them to do).

Note 2—But TOE says, 'Birds came from reptiles'.
This is rather like saying, 'Aeroplanes came from cars'.
Evolutionists have never yet answered these questions:
How did scales turn into feathers?
How did cold-blooded creatures become warm-blooded?
How did four legs become two legs?
How did heavy bones become light?
How did the reptiles practise flying? (jumping off a cliff?)
Everyone knows that an aeroplane has to be designed specially, and differently from a car, although *some* of the parts *look* similar.
The Wright Brothers (1903 A.D.) were successful with their heavier-than-air flying machine because it was designed and built *as a whole,* including their own light-weight petrol engine.
So, surely, the first birds must have been *from the beginning* perfectly adapted to flight—which is so utterly different from ground-movement.

Verses 20, 21, 22 and 23

Archaeopteryx

Note 3—The famous Archaeopteryx is supposed to be 'halfway between a reptile and a bird'; but in fact it is nothing of the sort. Having true wings and feathers, it was a real bird. Its teeth and wing-claws might be called 'reptilian', but that proves nothing. A South American bird called the Hoatzin has wing-claws;[49] so have some bats. And some reptiles are toothless. Some birds have gizzards, other have not. The woodpecker has a long tongue, but most birds do not. We might as well say that a woodpecker is 'halfway between a bird and an anteater' because of its long tongue, or that a chameleon is 'halfway between a lizard and a monkey' because of its hands and prehensile tail.

The fact is that in every Order (birds, fish, reptiles, etc.) God has created an enormous variety of likenesses and unlikenesses, but every creature reproduces only 'after its kind'.

Note 4—Many other questions are difficult for an Evolutionist to answer, e.g.

a. How did the tailor-bird of India acquire the skill to sew leaves together to form a nest?
How many thousands of eggs were smashed before they learned to do it *just right*?

Tailor bird

31

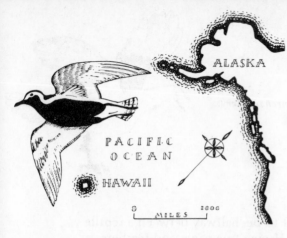

ALASKA

Migration of the golden plover

PACIFIC
OCEAN

HAWAII

0   MILES   1000

b. How do hundreds of species of birds annually migrate thousands of miles at the right time to the right place?

Every autumn the American Golden Plover youngsters fly 3000 miles across the Pacific from Alaska to the island of Hawaii, with no parent birds to guide them, through darkness, cloud and storms, and land plumb on target.

WHO taught the birds to navigate?[42]

c. Guillemots lay their eggs on bare windswept rock, but the eggs are so shaped that when the wind blows they simply revolve instead of rolling off. WHO taught the guillemot to produce eggs exactly the right shape, whereas other sea-birds build 'ordinary' nests?

(Research: find out how hornbills plan *their* nest—another marvel).

Note 5—The Hebrew word for 'bird' can be used for any flying thing, so here it probably includes (besides birds) flying insects, flying mammals (bats), and flying reptiles (pterodactyls).

TOE cannot account for any *one* of these groups 'evolving' from non-fliers, let alone for all four.

Note 7—There are two verses in the Book of Isaiah (14.29 and 30.6) which mention *flying serpents.* No such creature exists today, but the Greek historian Herodotus, who lived 200 years after Isaiah, gives a detailed description of flying serpents in Arabia[50] (Penguin Classics p.219), and we have no reason to doubt his word.

Once again the Bible agrees with *true science* (what has actually been observed by humans).

PROJECTS

1. What were the achievements of (a) Louis Agassiz?
                                   (b) Jean Henri Fabre?
   What was their attitude towards TOE? Why?

2. How did Louis Pasteur prove that life cannot come from non-life?

3. In what ways (beside the long tongue) do *woodpeckers* differ from other birds?
   Could these special features have 'happened' all together by chance?

4. Study the habits of *wasps* (a) social wasps
                                 (b) solitary wasps
   Can TOE account for these?

DAY SIX

Verse 24.   And God said, 'Let the earth bring forth living creatures after their kind: cattle and creeping things and beasts of the earth after their kind'; and it was so.

Note 1—Land creatures are here divided into three convenient groups according to common observation:

a—*Cattle* = (probably) sheep, oxen, donkeys, camels and horses, cats and dogs.

As far back as historical records go, these animals have always been 'tame'. There is no scentific evidence for the view that all animals were wild until domesticated by man. Rather, God knew man's needs and specially made some animals to help us (oxen for ploughing, sheep for clothing, horses for transport, etc.).

Many textbooks have a series of pictures showing how the *horse* is supposed to have 'evolved' from a small creature about the size of a terrier.

What the books do *not* tell you is that

i.—Nowhere on earth has anyone found these 'horse-ancestor' fossils lying on top of one another in regular order.

ii.—It is just as reasonable to believe that all these animals lived on earth at the same time, either as different species or as larger and smaller members of the same species (compare Great Danes and Dachshunds).

iii.—One modern breed of horse in Argentina averages only 17 inches in height. [17]

But Shire horses still weigh up to a ton, and Shetland ponies about one fifth of that.

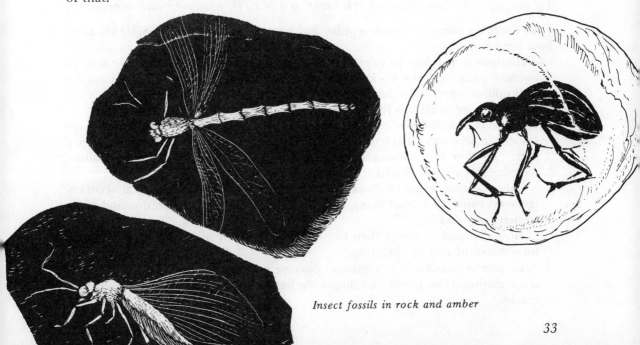

Insect fossils in rock and amber

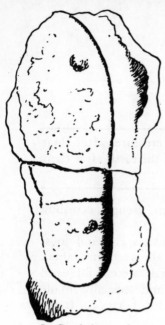
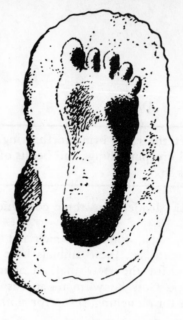
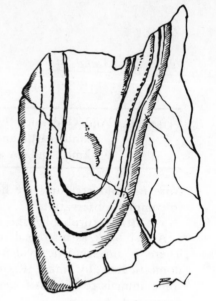

In Cambrian rock In Cretaceous rock (Paluxy River) In Triassic rock

Fossil human footprints[9]

  If all three types were to be found fossilized, TOE would tell us that 'horses gradually increased in size over millions of years'!—whereas in fact all three types are alive together in 1976.

iv.—No one has yet shown why small horses should become steadily larger by 'natural selection'. Just the opposite seems to have happened in the past: modern bears, tigers, turtles and many other animals are considerably *smaller* than their prehistoric 'relations'.

To sum up: *the 'evolution of the horse' is a MYTH,* unproven and unprovable.

  b—*Creeping things* = small reptiles and insects, of which some 800,000 kinds have been named.

i.—Evolution is at a loss to explain why *fossil insects look very much the same as modern ones,* e.g. the cockroach is supposed to have survived unchanged for 300 million years. Why has it not evolved into something better?

Some more questions (out of thousands) that TOE has never answered:

How did the 15,000 species of *ants* learn to organise their incredibly complicated society in so many different ways, e.g. carpenter ants, leaf-cutting ants, honey ants, harvester ants, cow-keeping ants, slave-making ants, army ants, fire ants—to name just a few? (WBE)

  How did *bees* learn to shape their cells with perfect mathematical accuracy (greatest capacity + least wax), and communicate distance, direction and wind-strength to other bees?[46]

  How did *spiders* evolve their five different kinds of silk and learn to use each for a different sort of operation?

  In several species (e.g. scorpion, praying mantis) the female kills the male after mating. How could this disgusting habit *increase* the survival power of a species?

34

ii.—*Reptiles* form a large class. Although their name means 'creeping' there is an amazing variety in their methods of movement. *Lizards,* for example: about 3000 different species. One kind can run at 18 miles per hour. Others move literally at snail's pace. The glass-snake (really a lizard) has a tail twice the length of its body. When an enemy grabs this tail, the lizard sheds it and starts growing another one. The chameleon, by contrast, has a roll-up tail for gripping twigs, independent eyes, and a tongue as long as his body. The horned 'toad', another lizard, can shoot blood out of his eyes for a distance of 3 feet. The gecko can draw in his claws (like a cat) and has a mass of hooks on his pad-feet which enable him to walk upside down on the ceiling.

All these very different and very special types of equipment are supposed to have evolved from some 'common ancestor'. But this hypothesis has never been proved: there are no fossil links.

Project—Find out how many varieties of SNAKE there are in the world. How many poisonous? how many non-poisonous?
Is it an advantage or a disadvantage for a snake to be poisonous?
If all snakes were originally poisonous, why did some become non-poisonous?
If all snakes were originally non-poisonous, why did some become poisonous?

Contemporary man and dinosaur

Female kangaroo

Answer—there is no evidence that any non-poisonous snake has ever become poisonous by 'natural selection', or that any poisonous snake has ever become non-poisonous. True science agrees with the Bible: God made each to reproduce only and always *according to its kind.* (In Chapter 3 we shall find out why God made some snakes poisonous).

   c—*Beasts of the earth* = wild animals which have no close connection with Man but roam freely.

i.—One of the most interesting discoveries of this century has been human foot-prints alongside *dinosaur* tracks in the Paluxy river-bed, Texas. This proves that man lived at the same time as the monsters, not 60 million years later as many scientists say.[9] (Other human footprints have been discovered in Utah, USA, crushing trilobites, which are supposed to be 500 million years old).[9]

ii.—Here we have space to include only one or two examples (out of thousands) of the marvellous complexity and variety of land-animals. Everyone knows that *kangaroos* have pouches. But did you know that only the females have them? (contrast the sea-horse, p.29). Also, when the 'joey' is born he needs milk, and to prevent the milk going into his lungs his windpipe is specially prolonged into the back of his nose. Could the joey's windpipe and the mother's pouch have 'evolved' together by chance?

iii—Some scientists believe that *penguins* were once flying birds, then 'somehow' lost the power of flight. But there are no fossils to support this idea, so we mention them here with land-animals. Some reptiles used to fly (see p.32) but most do not. Some insects fly and some do not. Most birds fly but some do not. All kinds seem happy with the powers they possess, and not in the least inclined to change them or lose them.

   Penguins, in particular, look pleased and playful if you watch a crowd of them cavorting on the ice. They are perfectly adapted to their peculiar way of life—diving, swimming, catching fish, nesting—and have almost certainly always been the same since 'the beginning'.

   The female Emperor penguin lays one egg on bare ice, then returns to the water.

The male keeps the egg warm between his feet and stomach for *two months without eating* through the worst part of the Antarctic winter.

When the chick hatches, the male feeds it with a milky substance produced in his throat.

Eventually mother returns, comfortably fat, and father goes to sea for three weeks, coming back with food for his family.

Does this 'planned parenthood' happen by chance?

Obviously, every chick penguin would have died long ago (like the tailor-bird babies, p.31) if its parents had not had the instinct to do things right *first time*.

iv.—By contrast, the mother *sea-turtle* takes no care whatever of her young. She simply digs a hole in the sand, lays her eggs, covers them, and scrambles back to sea. How does she know that the sun will hatch her eggs? and how does the penguin know the ice will *not* hatch hers? (For that matter, *how does any dumb creature know that eggs are important?*)

The only answer that makes sense is that God created 'all creatures great and small' perfectly adapted to their own environment and each endowed with instincts to do the right thing at the right time to ensure the survival of its offspring.

Verse 25b.   And God saw that it was good.

Notice that ten times in this chapter we have the words 'after its kind' or 'after their kinds'.

Darwin believed that small variations in each generation could add up to one kind of animal turning into another.

Since Darwin's day (1859) many scientists have conducted breeding experiments trying to prove he was right—but without success.

a—*Dogs* have an enormous range in size and shape, from the huge Irish wolfhound to the tiny Chihuahua—but they are still dogs.

b—*Fruitflies* can be changed in all sorts of ways by radiation, but they still remain fruitflies.

c—If a donkey is crossed with a mare, a *mule* is born.

But if you want another mule you must repeat the process—

because all male mules are sterile: they cannot reproduce.

In nature crossbreeds just don't happen. Mr Sparrow is not interested in Miss Robin.

And when crossbreeds are produced artificially in zoos (e.g. a lioness crossed with a tiger), they will almost always be sterile.

d—Among the *pepper-moths* of North England, those best survive which have the best camouflage, but they never change into butterflies.

So scientific research agrees with the Bible:

God made each kind of creature, and *variation is possible only within the kind.*

DID GOD WORK THROUGH EVOLUTION?

Some people say,

'It would be *more wonderful* for God to make a machine that produces one thing out of another—

than to make each living thing separately.

Therefore evolution is *more wonderful* than special creation,

therefore evolution from amoeba to man is true!'

Let us carefully examine this idea.

We shall find that it includes at least three serious errors.

ERROR NO.1: Wonderful events are not necessarily true events.

About 50–100 years after the New Testament Gospels were written, people began making up stories about Jesus. Thus we have a 'Gospel of Peter' (*not* written by Peter), a 'Gospel of Thomas', and several others. They include many bogus 'miracles': for instance the story of how Jesus as a boy made mud sparrows, then clapped his hands—and they flew away. This story is 'more wonderful' than anything Matthew, Mark, Luke and John tell us about Jesus' boyhood—but that doesn't make it true.

The only *true* record of Christ's miracles is contained in those books which have always and everywhere been accepted by Christians; and the only *true* record of God's miracles 'in the beginning' is contained in those books which have always and everywhere been accepted by God's people, the Jews.

ERROR NO.2: God is not a Grand Magician who pulls rabbits out of hats, bats out of mice, or men out of monkeys, in order to gain our applause.

The God of the Bible is a God of Law and Order.

We are called to praise Him not for conjuring tricks but for the fantastic miracle of instant-creation:

'Let all the earth fear the Lord . . .

For He spoke and it was done!' (Psalm 33.8).

ERROR NO.3: If Evolution is said to be like a factory, with Man as the end-product, then God must be the most inefficient, stupid and wasteful factory-builder that ever existed.

According to evolutionists, millions of 'experimental' animals have been produced, only to die off when conditions changed.

For instance, the dinosaurs.

What conceivable purpose was served by these huge reptiles roaming the earth for scores of millions of years?

But *God is not wasteful nor stupid nor inefficient:*

a—Jesus told the disciples to gather up the left-over pieces, *not* to waste them.

b—He never lost one hour of one day (John 9.5; 11.9), let alone a year.

c—Every recorded miracle was done perfectly, first time.

So, from all we know about God from other parts of the Bible, it seems most unlikely that He produced this world by means of evolution.

Dinosaurs, brachiosaurus and ornithomimus

(The 'mystery' of the dinosaurs' existence and destruction will be solved when we come to Genesis 6—8).

Verse 26.   **And God said, 'Let us make man in our image, according to our like-ness: and let them rule over the fish of the sea and over the birds of the sky, and over the cattle, and over all the earth, and every creeping thing that creeps upon the earth'.**

Verse 27.   **And God created man in His own image, in the image of God He created him;**

Note 1—These verses show the supreme importance of Man, as distinct from the animals:
a—God made a special plan and decision before creating man.
b—Man was made like God in his powers of reasoning, planning, imagining, creating (music, literature, pictures), knowing right from wrong, and speaking.
c—Man was made to govern the world for God.

OBJECTION
'All modern scientists agree that Man evolved from Monkey, or a monkey-like ancestor'.

Note 2—In the past 50 years, scores of books have been written to show that this statement is untrue. You will find some of them listed in our bibliography. Perhaps the best short answer is:
The Creation Research Society, founded in 1963, has over 1000 members, all scientists with at least two University degrees, and *none* of them believe that Man has evolved!

Let us now consider some of the reasons which have led these scientists to reject Darwin's theory and to accept Genesis One as the true account of man's origin. It will be convenient to refer to a recent publication by a modern evolutionist, Dr M. H. Day, who is Reader in Physical Anatomy at the Middlesex Hospital, London. His book is entitled *'FOSSIL MAN'*[30] (Hamlyn all-colour paperback) (1969).

REASON No.1: Dr Day *assumes the very thing he sets out to prove.*
The back-cover blurb states:
   'This book traces the evolution of Man and his changes in body . . .'
Now, you can only 'trace' something that really exists.
You cannot (e.g.) 'trace' or track the Abominable Snowman until you know it is *he* that has made the footprints.
Before you know that, you can only examine the evidence.
And you may come to the conclusion that the Abominable Snowman is only a popular legend!
So with Evolution. It is *bad science* to pretend that a case is already proved, when Dr Day himself admits (p.155):
   'What is known of the evolution of man is still but a fraction of what there is yet to learn'.
   CRS scientists have examined the actual evidence and have come to the conclusion that Evolution is only a popular legend.

REASON No.2: The same blurb in the same paragraph *uses the word 'evolution' in two totally different senses:*
1—to describe the changes in man's body, which (according to TOE) came entirely at random and by chance;
2—to describe man's own improvements of his own technology (tool-making, art, etc.), each one deliberately planned and carefully worked out.
   This confusion in the use of words is again *bad science.*

REASON No.3: The front cover of *'FOSSIL MAN'* carries an imaginative drawing of an 'Ape-man', with long black head-hair, greenish-brown skin, body-hair not much shorter than an ape's, thick lips, ape-like ears, and prominent teeth. The *impression given* is that we know what 'Apemen' looked like. But there is no scientific evidence that such a creature ever existed! The picture has been concocted by a clever artist from a few teeth, or part of a skull, perhaps a shin bone, plus a huge slice of imagination.
   Consider the differences between a lion and a tiger: even a two-year old can tell them apart. But when they are dead and buried, and their skeletons are dug up, they look almost identical. Few Professors of Zoology would risk a bet on which was which. In other words, it is impossible to tell from *bones* what was the colour of the animal's skin, length and colour of hair and whiskers, shape of nose, ears, etc., even when dealing with well-known animals.
   From this we may judge how *unscientific it is to pretend to know what a*

'fossil man' looked like, when nobody in the world has ever seen a single specimen. Even if the whole skeleton were intact—which it rarely is—it would be quite impossible to tell the colour of his skin, the length or colour of his hair (if any) on head or body, the shape of his ears or nose. Even teeth are no sure guide to eating habits. (Inside the front cover is another sub-human eating raw meat off the bone. There is no evidence whatever for this, since evolutionists admit that man used fire 500,000 B.C.). So this again is *bad science.* It is fact confused with fiction. The unwary reader is misled by an unscientific picture on the front cover and an unscientific use of words on the back cover.

REASON No.4: Evolutionists tend to overlook, omit or ignore all evidence unfavourable to their theory.
    There are at least three examples of this in *'FOSSIL MAN'.*

1—Dr Day has nothing but praise for Eugene Dubois, the Dutchman who discovered 'Java Man' in 1891. We are not told the facts: that Dubois also discovered the Wadjak (truly human) skulls at the same level as 'Java Man', but concealed them for 30 years because he wanted his first discovery to be admired as a 'missing link'; and before he died Dubois confessed, or at least gave his opinion, that 'Java Man' was really a gibbon (monkey)![15] Nor are we told of Frau Selenka's expedition in 1907 which found that the area of Dubois' discoveries was volcanic in origin, so that Java Man could not be more than 500 years old.[51]

2—The fossils of real men have been discovered (in Italy and California) at lower levels than any so-called ape-men. This of course proves that humans must be as old or older than 'ape-men' and cannot be descended from them.[26] But Dr Day *makes no mention whatever of these skulls.* Once again this is *bad science,* because if a theory is true it will explain all the facts, not just a selected few.

3—The true story of 'Peking Man' is a grand international mix-up.
    Starting from one tooth which a Canadian doctor claimed came from a brand new line of 'ape-men', the tale runs through the 1920s and 1930s with Austrian, Swedish, Chinese, French, German and Australian experts all putting forward contradictory theories of who or what Peking Man was. Finally in World War II all the fossil bones were lost, so now *there is no first-hand evidence available,* only plaster casts of some of the bones, and 'flesh models' of what one expert thought Peking Man ought to have looked like. The final verdict was pronounced in 1968 by a Chinese-speaking Irishman who had lived in China throughout the discovery period. After carefully studying all the reports in English and Chinese he concludes that 'Peking Man' was *another fraud:* the skulls belonged to monkeys which had been killed and eaten by real *men* who used the hillside for *lime-burning.*[33/34]
    Dr Day, however, in his book published a year later (1969), ignores all these problems and contradictions. He prints (p.111) a romantic picture of two-legged *monkeys* with long hair and human hands building a fire *to ward off wild animals.* What does this picture prove? That artistic imagination is a wonderful gift—but very bad science.

(The most famous fake of all, 'Piltdown Man', fooled all the world's fossil experts for 40 years.[29] Teilhard de Chardin, who is believed by many to have been the faker, also played a part in the discovery of 'Peking Man').

Putting it all together we may truly say that Dr Day's *'FOSSIL MAN'* is clever *propaganda for the religion of Darwinism,* but does not present a single FACT which should cause us to doubt the Bible.

Verse 27b.   Male and female He created them.

Note 1—Notice that only in the creation of humans is there any mention of male and female. Obviously all other creatures were made male and female too, so there must be some special reason.

This special reason is explained more fully in Chapter 2.18—25.

Eve was created in a special way—out of Adam—not just to have babies, but to be Adam's helper and companion.

Note 2—Science has no adequate answer to the question, How did sex evolve?—either in humans or animals.

The process of reproduction is marvellously complex, and must have been perfect from the beginning to be successful.

Note 3—Scientists used to think that the microscopic 'paramoecium' would be very simple because it is so small.

We now know that this 'simple' organism has twenty different sexes![45]

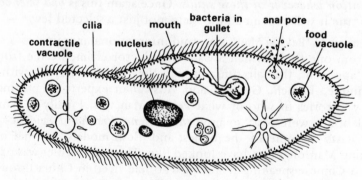

Paramoecium

Note 4—All other creatures were made (probably) in large numbers, but the human race began with *one pair only.*

This account is confirmed by Science. All races of men can intermarry, and children of 'mixed' race can in their turn have children of their own (unlike the mule). This shows that, as St. Paul said, we are ONE race and of ONE blood, whatever the colour of our skin (Acts 17.26).

Verses 26, 27, 27b and 28

Note 5—This idea of all-humans-one-race was quite *un*familiar in the ancient world. For example the Athenians liked to call themselves 'autochthones' which means 'sprung from the soil' of Greece, and despised all non-Greeks as 'barbarians'. The ancient Jews, too, were exceedingly proud of their ancestry and would never have invented a story which put them on a level with the 'heathen'. But they dared not change God's word.

Verse 28.   And God blessed them; and God said, 'Be fruitful and multiply, and fill the earth and subdue it; and rule over the fish of the sea, and over the birds of the air, and over every living thing that moves on the earth'.

Note 2—It is God's will that married couples should have children. Abortion and contraception are unnatural, and contrary to the clear command of God.

Note 2—After Adam sinned, man lost much of his authority over the animals. Some people have succeeded in 'staring out' tigers, but many more have been eaten by them.

Note 3—*Population statistics* show that the Bible dates of Creation and the Flood are much more reasonable than TOE's dates.

The present doubling rate of the world's population is about once every 40 years.

Suppose we allow that it may have been much slower in the past—say once every 500 years.

Then after 500 years there would have been 4 people	
after 1000 years	8
1500	16
2000	32
2500	64
3000	128
3500	256
4000	512
4500	1024
5000	2048

So the original pair would have multiplied by (roughly) 1000 in 5000 years. But TOE says that man has been on earth at least one hundred times longer than this, i.e. 500,000 years.

If this were so, the population today would be 2×1000^{100}, i.e. a thousand followed by three hundred zeros.

There would be no standing room for such a crowd on this planet.

In other words, if you accept TOE as true, you come up with a fantastically impossible result.

But if the Flood took place around 2500 B.C. we get a doubling rate of about once every 160 years, which is quite reasonable.[39]

Verse 29.   **And God said, 'Behold, I have given you every plant yielding seed which is on the surface of all the earth, and every tree that has fruit yielding seed; it shall be food for you;**

Verse 30.   **and to every beast of the earth and to every bird of the sky and to every thing that moves on the earth which has life, I have given every green plant for food'; and it was so.**

Note 1—When God first made the world, every bird and land-animal was vegetarian (fishes are not mentioned, so we can't be sure about them). Is this possible? Well, consider—

a—The largest dinosaurs were, and all elephants are, herbivores. Lions bred in captivity have thrived on a vegetarian diet. Dogs, cats, bears, and many other carnivores (flesh-eaters) can get along very well without meat.

b—Genesis 3.14 indicates that the snake and perhaps other animals were *changed* after Adam's sin.

So lions, tigers etc. may at first have had different jaws, different digestive systems, and a different nature, suited to a vegetarian diet.

c—We know from the Bible that God is love (I John 4.8).

So He must hate to see pain and suffering, far more than we do.

When He first made the world, there was no need for any animal to prey on any other,

there was *no* pain, *no* suffering, *no* disease and *no* death (at least for humans). 'Nature red in tooth and claw' was made so only *after Genesis 3*.

Verse 31.   **And God saw everything that He had made, and behold, it was very good.**

Note 1—The words 'very good' draw our attention to the finished perfection of God's work, seen as a whole.

Someone has said, 'If the stars came out only one night in a century, the whole world would turn out that night and stare and stare and marvel at their beauty, tell it to their children and grandchildren. But because it happens *every* night, nobody cares or stares!'

This is true of every part of God's creation.

There is more of miracle in the tiniest flower than in the tallest skyscraper.

Note 2—Even now, Darwin's idea of all life being a 'struggle for survival' is a very one-sided opinion.

Verses 28, 29, 30 and 31

Passenger pigeons

By far the cruellest predator (preying animal) is Man:

a—Before the coming of the white man, sixty million bison roamed the plains of North America. In the C.19th they were wantonly slaughtered until only a few hundred remained.

b—Similarly in 1800 A.D. passenger pigeons were numbered by the thousand million (in the U.S.A.), but in 1914 the last survivor of this species died in a zoo.

Today Wild Life Campaigners are trying to save the whale, the tiger, and many other over-hunted animals from the same fate.

But remember—it is a campaign against *man's* cruelty, not God's.

Note 3—Though dogs occasionally quarrel over a bone, most wild creatures do not fight each other to get food.

Tigers and leopards set themselves boundaries in the jungle and do not normally encroach on each other's territory. *Only* man is insatiably greedy for more land, more pleasure and more power.

Note 4—Listen to the birds' chorus on a May morning, and ask yourself:

'Does this sound like a struggle for survival, or a hymn of praise?'

Without doubt, the vast majority of God's creatures ENJOY life even in this sin-cursed world:

'You open Your hand and satisfy the desire of every living thing'. Psalm 145.16.

Note 5—So it is not hard to believe that, before Adam sinned, ALL living things enjoyed life ALWAYS.

SUMMING UP

The Bible presents us with a picture of planned perfection—earth, sky, sea, plants, sun-moon-and-stars, fishes, birds, animals, Man and Woman: the world a perfect environment for man, and man perfectly equipped to rule the world for God.

A world of infinite variety, beauty and harmony;

A world of warm days, yet never too hot,
    and cool nights, yet never too cold.

A world of work without weariness, and food gathered without toil.

Above all, a world without greed, lust, jealousy, hatred or fear; a world of peace, love and friendship between God and man. Such was the shining perfection of our world as originally designed and created.

OBJECTION

'Surely the most important message of Genesis One is:
    it tells us WHO created the world, rather than HOW he did it?'

Answer—In any book, as in any class lesson, we can best judge the importance of a subject by the number of times it is *repeated*.

Let us apply this test to the chapter we have just read.

10 times: **'God said . . .'** The most important lesson is God's *creation* of all things out of nothing. (This contradicts the idea of some scientists that Matter is eternal).

7 times: **'God saw that it was good.'** The second most important lesson is the *perfection* of God's original creation. (This contradicts the 'scientific' story of millions of years of animal slaughter, experiment and extinction, disease, disaster and death).

6 times: **'And there was evening and there was morning . . .'** The third most important lesson is that this whole marvellous work took *only six days*. To emphasise this point, God included these words in the only direct written message He has ever sent to man (Exodus 20.11).

PROJECT

One other phrase occurs 10 times in this chapter.
    a) What is it?
    b) How does it contradict TOE?

GENESIS CHAPTER TWO

Focus on Eden — Mind and memory, chimps and chess — History, mystery, or myth? — Adam's intelligence — God's midwifery — Eve's beauty.

Verse 1. **Thus the heavens and the earth were finished and all the host of them.**

Q.—Could God really have made everything in six days?

Answer—If there is a God at all, He could have made everything in six seconds or a sixtieth of a second.

Q.—Then why did He take six days?

Answer—In order to set us an example of measured, planned, orderly WORK, followed by one day of REST.

Objection—Science tells us that the earth took millions of years to cool down and for life to evolve to its present stage.

Answer—Science cannot tell how long men took to build the Great Pyramid or Stonehenge, even when it is known where the materials came from.

Science cannot make a single blade of grass or a microbe, even when all the materials are available.

How then can scientists possibly tell how, or how long, God took to make EVERYTHING out of NOTHING?

Note—If you study the Gospels you will find that nearly all Christ's miracles were *instantaneous*.

This is the way that God works—not in years, but in NO TIME! (Similarly, I Corinthians 15.52 says that at the end of the world Christians' bodies will be changed 'in a moment', which means in a fraction of time *indivisibly small*).

CHANGE AND CHANCE

Some scientists say that the probability of our world having evolved by chance is about as great as the probability of an explosion in a printing press producing the Encyclopaedia Britannica complete in 24 volumes.

But other scientists argue: 'A monkey tapping away at random on a typewriter would eventually write correctly not only words but also phrases, sentences, and even whole books. *So,* given enough time, "chance" can produce anything—whales, bees, spiders, monkeys, Man.'

Answer—Let us assume that the monkey uses a typewriter with 60 keys: 26 small letters, 26 capitals, a space, full stop, comma, colon, semicolon, two brackets and a question mark.

Suppose we wish the monkey to produce the word *Peanut.* Now, the chances of the monkey typing the letter P are 1:60, and of typing Pe 1/60 x 1/60 = 1 in 3600.

So his chances of typing the six-letter word Peanut are $(1/60)^6$ = 1 in 46,656,000,000.

This means that if the monkey could type at a rate of 3 letters per second, he would have to type for 450 years to produce 'Peanut'.

Now let's take the phrase 'Peanuts and Typewriters' (just 23 correct letters and spaces). This would take a million monkeys over a thousand million million million million years (i.e. 10^{27} years), each typing away at 3 letters per second.

This time period is a hundred thousand million million (i.e. 10^{17}) times as long as the age of the universe according to the Theory of Evolution. And it is needed for only *23* letters and spaces to be put together correctly!

But our world contains many more than 23 things correctly put together; so it would take inconceivably longer still for these hundreds and thousands of things to get together correctly 'by chance'.

This is why a good number of scientists in recent years have been calling Darwin's theory 'mathematical *nonsense*'. 5000 million years is nothing like enough time for random evolution.[26]

Verse 2.   **And on the seventh day God finished His work which He had done, and he rested on the seventh day from all His work which He had done.**

Verse 3.   **So God blessed the seventh day, and hallowed it, because on it God rested from all His work which He had done in creation.**

Note 1—Historians are puzzled to know who invented the seven-day week.

It does not fit exactly into the solar year of 365¼ days nor into the moon-month of 29 days.

Where did it come from?
The simplest answer is—from God.

Note 2—Experience has proved it to be by far the most satisfactory way of organizing man's life, in every century and in every country of the world.

Verses 1, 2 and 3

The French Revolutionaries tried to abolish it
so did the Russian Revolutionaries
so did the Government of Sri Lanka (Ceylon) in the 1960s—
but in the end they all had to bring it back.
One rest day in eight is too long an interval—
one day in six is too short—
one day in seven is *just right.*

Note 3—Objection: 'The Jews invented the sabbath (rest) day.'

Answer: this seems most unlikely, because the Jews repeatedly broke the law and resented it.
The prophet Amos accuses them of grumbling:

'When will the sabbath be over, so that we may offer wheat for sale?'

You won't find schoolchildren making up school rules to cut down their own freedom!

Verse 4.   These are the generations of the heaven and the earth when they were created, in the day that the Lord God made earth and heaven.

Note 1—The first four words of this verse are repeated *ten times* in Genesis.
We have the 'generations' of Adam, Noah, Shem . . . Esau and Jacob.
This seems to show that 'generations' really means 'history'.
So here it shows that the story of Creation is literal *history* as much as the later stories of Joseph, Jacob and Esau etc.

It is not a hymn or a poem or a parable or a fable.
It is not science-fiction, but FACT!

Note 2—The word 'day' is here used in a wide general sense meaning 'time'. (But Hebrew never uses 'day' with a *number* to mean anything other than 24 hours).

FOCUS ON MAN

Note 1—We now have a CLOSE-UP of the most important of all God's creatures—Man.
Often a film begins with a wide sweep of country or city—a PANORAMA. Genesis One + ch.2.1—3 is such a panorama: a view of all creation at a glance. Genesis Two 4—25 is a close-up showing *details*.

Note 2—For 3000 years no Hebrew scholar doubted that Genesis 1 and 2 were written by the same man, and make sense together.
Then about 200 years ago some French and German scholars tried to prove that

a—ch.1 contradicts ch.2, so they cannot have been written by the same author;

b—both chapters were written long after Moses' time.

Other (equally clever) modern scholars have shown that

a—there is no contradiction at all between chapters 1 and 2, which tell the same story, but from different viewpoints;

b—there is no reason to doubt that Moses wrote or compiled both chapters.

Note 3—Jesus in one breath quoted words from *both* chapters as making sense *together:*

> 'Have you not read that He who made them from the beginning made them male and female (ch.1) and said (ch.2), For this cause a man shall leave his father and mother, and shall be joined to his wife; and the two shall become one flesh?' (Matthew 19.4—5)

and He implies that *both* sentences are *the words of the Creator.*

Verse 7.   And the Lord God formed man of the dust of the ground, and breathed into his nostrils the breath of life, and man became a living soul.

Note 1—Notice the Bible says clearly that God used *non-living* stuff (earth) to make man into a *living* soul.

'Soul' is the same Hebrew word as 'creature' in ch.1.21,24, so the writer cannot mean that God took a (monkey-like) creature which already existed, and made *that* into a man.

The words can only mean that Adam was created directly from inorganic material in an instant,

not from an Ape or Ape-man which had been 'evolving' for millions of years.

Note 2—Here are some more questions to which TOE has no satisfactory answer:

a—Apes are quadrupeds (walking on four feet), man alone of mammals walks on two feet.

How did the ape-man survive for millions of years tottering around in the very uncomfortable *half-bent* position?

No fossils of such a creature have ever been found.

Apes are quadrupeds — gorilla walking

b—In a human foot the five toes are all bound together by *one* muscle, so the human big toe cannot grip at all strongly.

But an ape grips mainly with his big toe, using it like a thumb with a separate muscle.

How could the four-toes-and-a-thumb foot gradually become a five-toes-in-a-line foot? The ape-man with only a half-toe grip would have fallen off the branch and broken his neck.

Again—*no fossils* of any intermediate stage.

c—*Why should an ape or ape-man gradually become more intelligent?* There is no evidence that ANY species of animal has become more intelligent over the centuries.

Fossil animals are generally BIGGER than modern animals, so (if intelligence can be measured by brain-size), modern apes are probably *less* intelligent than prehistoric apes.

And of course it is well known that Cro-Magnon Man (dated 20,000 B.C.) had a BIGGER brain than most of us in the C20th A.D. Why?

Note 3—Man's brain is actually smaller than a whale's or an elephant's, but no scientist would deny that man's *mind* is 1000 times more intelligent.

Or, if you go by the ratio of brain-weight to body-weight, man's brain makes up only 2.5% of his total weight,

whereas a sparrow's brain is 4.2% of its total weight.

This shows that man is a different *kind* of creature.

> ONLY man has a sense of right and wrong
>> prays and worships
>> buries his dead
>> believes in a Life after Death.

Note 4—But even apart from man's *spiritual* nature, the powers of man's mind show that the gap separating him from the apes is 'practically infinite'. (We shall look at the very important matter of language in chapter 11). Two other examples:

a—*MUSIC.* You probably know scores of pop-songs.

Most church-goers know hundreds of hymn-tunes.

And a good concert-pianist knows *thousands of pages* of music by heart.

In the 1880s an American Negro, who was born blind, astounded audiences all over Europe by playing a vast repertoire of piano concertos etc. *without ever having seen a note!*

How would a chimpanzee compare with this?

He can't even sing one tune, let alone play or remember it.

b—*CHESS.* Are you a player?

Perhaps you find it difficult, but almost anyone can learn.

With 64 squares and 32 pieces the possible number of moves in any one game runs into millions. In spite of this some Grand Masters are able to play several games at once *blindfold.* (Someone tells him the other man's move, then he has to remember it).

In 1951 George Koltanowski, a (still living) Polish-American, played 50 opponents at once, blindfolded. He won 43 games, lost 2 and drew 3.[52] The powers of memory involved in a feat like this are simply staggering.

What about the chimp?

So far as we know, even the abstract idea of one 'rule' governing the movement of one pawn is *completely beyond him.*

Note 5—Chemically speaking, every element of man's body can be found in the earth, so it is literally true that man is composed 'of the dust of the ground'.

Project: (1) Find out how many different species there are of (a) monkeys (b) apes. Which are better 'adapted to their environment'?

(2) If their 'common ancestor' had a tail, how/why did the apes *lose* their tails?

If their 'common ancestor' had no tail, how/why did monkeys *get* tails? one vertebra at a time?

Verse 5.   Now no shrub of the field was yet in the earth, and no plant of the field had yet sprouted,

for the Lord God had not sent rain upon the earth, and there was no man to cultivate the ground.

Note 1—This verse has puzzled many people because it *seems* to contradict what we have been told in Chapter One, that vegetation was created before Man.

(*Hint:* whenever you think you have found a contradiction or mistake in the Bible, *take a second look.* For 2000 years clever people have hammered away at this Book, but in the end it is always the clever people who are proved wrong.)

Why be an ape?

Verses 7, 5 and 8

Note 2—The best explanation seems to be:

      shrub-of-the-field = thorn bushes (Job 30.4,7: Genesis 21.15)

      plant-of-the-field = cereals (wheat, oats etc.)

   Neither of these phrases are used in ch.1, and probably neither of these kinds of vegetation grew until *after God's curse* on the ground. Before the Curse, man ate only fruit, but after Gen.3.19 he had to sweat at ploughing, reaping etc.

Note 3—According to EB: 'the origin of cereals is still a mystery to C.20th biologists', so science makes no claim to have a better explanation.

Note 4—The point of this verse is: before describing the beautiful Garden of Eden, the writer wishes to emphasise how different (i.e. how much *better)* the earth was before Sin and the Curse.

Verse 8.   And the Lord God planted a garden eastward, in Eden;
and there He put the man whom He had formed.

Note 1—Where was the Garden of Eden? Did it ever exist?

   All we are told is that it was east of Palestine (Israel) or Sinai, where Moses edited these ancient records.

   The Flood must have changed much of the landscape of the Middle East, but you can still find Euphrates and Tigris (= Hiddekel v.14) on a map of Iraq.

HISTORY, MYSTERY, OR MYTH?

Most people enjoy Fairy Tales. We know Jack's Giant didn't really fall off the Beanstalk, and Cinderella's pumpkin could not really turn into a carriage; but we get a warm comfortable *feeling* inside of us by just thinking that cruelty will be punished and goodness rewarded.

   Now—some scholars believe that the story of Adam and Eve is a kind of fairy tale, just made up to give us the right *feelings* about God, animals, marriage and sex. They call it a Myth, and they say that myths can be 'true' in a way because e.g. in the real world, disobedience is often punished and obedience rewarded.

   Other scholars point out that

a—wherever in the Bible we find parables or fables—that is, stories made up to teach a lesson—we are always told that they *are* parables (e.g. Luke 8.14; 15.3; 18.1,9); *or* it is quite obvious that the story is not meant to be taken literally (e.g. Judges 9.8—20).

b—here there is nothing to show that the Garden of Eden story is a parable or fable;

c—in the NT Adam is mentioned nine times and Eve four times, each time as *real persons,* e.g. St Paul says:

      'Adam was first formed, then Eve'
      the woman was created for the man' (I Tim.2.13; I Cor.11.9).

d—The writer mentions *15 geographical facts* in connection with Eden, and eleven of these are in the present tense (e.g. 'the gold of that land *is* good'). Nobody now knows exactly where are or were Pishon, Havilah, Gihon or Cush, but obviously they were real to the writer. So there is every reason to believe that Eden was a *real* garden with *real* rivers, *real* trees and *real* fruit, either in Armenia (eastern Turkey) or in Iraq.

Conclusion: Like every other chapter of Genesis (except ch.49, which is Poetry), these chapters are not Myth but *History*.

Verse 9.   And out of the ground the Lord God made to grow every tree that is pleasant to the sight and good for food . . .

Note 1—Once again, there is no contradiction between this verse and 1.11.

All kinds of fruit tree were already growing *somewhere* in the world, but God selected those that were specially beautiful and had the most delicious taste, and planted them—perhaps in orderly rows—in the garden.

Note 2—We tend to think of 'Nature' as *dis*orderly. If you landed on a desert island and found fields with hedges laid out in exact squares, or trees planted in exact circles, you would immediately think:

'Some *human* has been here'.

You would probably be right, because *now* God has left us to toil at subduing the earth and taming the wilderness.

But God is still a God of Law and Order. Every snowflake He makes is a perfect hexagon, and every blood corpuscle exactly the right shape to combine maximum absorbing speed with maximum strength.[47]

So it would have been no trouble at all for Him to lay out an orderly garden. In fact, of course, man's natural 'instinct' for symmetry, order and organization, simply proves the Bible statement that we are 'made in the image of God'.

Verse 15.   And the Lord God took the man and put him into the garden of Eden to cultivate and keep it.

Note 1—Note the repetition from v.8.

This does not mean that two different writers told the story.

The Greek poet Homer was one of the best story-tellers that ever lived, and he often repeats important lines.

Note 2—The first man was not a cave-man but a gardener.

Men took to living in caves, and hunting, only *after* the (probable) change of climate that followed Adam's sin.

Note 3—It is impossible to tell what kind of garden-tools Adam used, but we do know that Early Man was able to make exceedingly sharp stone instruments.

Verses 16, 17   And the Lord God commanded the man, saying, 'Of every tree
of the garden you may freely eat:
but of the tree of the knowledge of good and evil you shall *not*
eat, for in the day that you eat of it, you shall surely die.'

Note 1—Man is the only creature on earth knowing the difference between right
and wrong, and having the power freely to choose between them.

You can train rats not to eat cheese (by giving them an electric shock when
they nibble it),
but you can never get into a rat's head the idea: 'it is WRONG to steal cheese'.

Note 2—Why did God not allow Adam to eat EVERY fruit?
Did He want to make Adam miserable?

Answer—No. God wanted Adam to be perfectly happy.

And God knows what makes up perfect happiness:
we creatures can only be happy in OBEDIENCE to our Creator.

Note 3—*Objection:*
'Nowadays even murderers get only a few years prison sentence for their crime.
Isn't the DEATH PENALTY rather tough just for eating a fruit?'

Answer:
a—It is as useless to quarrel with the Law of God as to quarrel with the law of
   electricity,
You only have to touch a high-tension cable once, and you will be dead.
   There is no second chance.
b—God's law laid down the DEATH PENALTY for one sin, but God's love sent
   down Jesus to pay that penalty for all our billion sins.

Verse 18.   And the Lord God said, 'It is not good that the man should be alone:
I will make him a helper fit for him.'

Note 1—Notice that God did not say, 'The man needs children, I will make him a
mate'. The first and most important reason for Woman's creation was that Man
should have a *helper* and companion.

This contradicts Women's Lib *and* Women's Slavery *and* polygamy (having
more than one wife).
(In some countries even now girls are bought and sold,
   and a woman is *cheaper than a cow.*
At the time when Genesis was written, this sort of thing was common all over the
world.

Only the Jewish Scriptures showed the right relationship between men and
women.)

NAMING OF THE ANIMALS

Verse 19. And out of the ground the Lord God (had) formed every beast of the field, and every bird of the sky, and He brought them to the man to see what he (Adam) would call them:
and whatever the man called every living creature, that was its name.

Note 1—This verse does not contradict 1.24, which says that birds and animals were created before man. Hebrew has no pluperfect tense ('had'), so we must put it in to make sense in English.

(Alternatively, some scholars think God specially created *some* birds and animals in the Garden, for the Garden—i.e. hundreds rather than thousands. It is difficult, for instance, to imagine how many pairs of brontosauri could have been comfortably accommodated in Eden, and Eden still be called a Garden!)

Note 2—Probably the writer repeats 'out of the ground' to remind us that animals and birds were made in an *entirely different way* from Eve.

Verse 20. And the man gave names to all cattle, and to the birds of the sky, and to every beast of the field; but for man there was not found a helper fit for him.

Note 1—Adam's *superb intelligence:* he did something no other man has ever done or could ever do.

It is said that in World War II the Captain of one cruiser could remember the names of all 700 of his crew after calling the roll *just once.*

That was remarkable.

But Adam had to invent names for at least 3500 mammals, 8600 birds, and 5500 reptiles and amphibians, and *remember what he had called them!*

Note 2—How could he do this?

Answer—Adam was a better man than we are, so he had a better mind.

He was better because he was perfect—without SIN.
Sin not only spoils our bodies, by disease and decay:
it also spoils our powers of learning, memory, imagination and invention.

Note 3—Adam's *language* must have been implanted in his mind from the beginning as an 'instinct', like a bird's instinct to build a nest. (We shall discuss this important matter again in ch.11).

Animals (e.g. monkeys) have different sounds to express joy, fear, etc. but no monkey can communicate to another the idea
        'Fear—leopard!'
as a different idea from   'Fear—snake!'

Verses 19, 20, 21 and 22

On the other hand even the most 'primitive' tribes use very complicated languages with a vocabulary of scores of thousands of words. (One South Sea Island language has 14 different words to describe a coconut palm at different stages of its growth).[58]

Note 4—Could Adam have named all the animals and birds in one day?

(Of course if we accept the alternative suggested under v.19 (1), there is no problem.)

This *seems* to be implied, because we know from 1.27 that Eve was created on Day 6.

Answer—the Bible is a 'condensed book' and we must use common-sense in interpreting it.

When we read that Solomon 'spoke 3000 proverbs: and his songs were 1005 . . . and he spoke of trees . . . beasts, and of birds, and of creeping things, and of fishes', we do not picture him giving a Royal Recital lasting days or weeks. It means that Solomon knew all those things and spoke of them from time to time.

So perhaps **verse 20** can be interpreted to mean that Adam *began* to name the animals on Day 6, but it wasn't long before he realised his own need of a mate. Then Eve was created; then Adam completed his task of naming.

Note 5—Adam's *authority* over the animals and birds is implied here, (i.e. they were all 'tame') as well as God's *control* in bringing them to him in an orderly manner (compare 6.20 where God did the same for Noah).

Jesus used the same kind of control when He brought fish into Peter's net (Luke 5) and directed one particular fish to be hooked on Peter's line (Matthew 17).

Verse 21.   **And the Lord God caused a deep sleep to fall upon Adam, and he slept; and God took one of Adam's ribs, and closed up its place with flesh:**

Verse 22.   **And the rib which the Lord God had taken from the man, He made into a woman.**

Note 1—Here we have the first MIDWIFERY OPERATION in history:
  the patient was a man
  the surgeon/anaesthetist was God
  and the result was a full-grown woman!

Q.—How did God do an operation without instruments?

Answer—a—Jesus healed the nobleman's son at a distance of several miles (John 4.50) without instruments or medicine.

God is a Spirit, but obviously He can do without hands or instruments anything that we can do with them.

57

b—Another good example is the two slabs of stone given to Moses (Exodus 31.18).

God cut them out of the mountain and wrote on them the Ten Commandments, but He didn't need a chisel.

Note 2—Anaesthetics were not invented till the 1840s, at least 3000 years after Genesis was written. (Queen Victoria was the first woman in history to have a baby under chloroform, in 1853).

How could any writer B.C. possibly have guessed God's method of creating Eve?

We now know that anaesthesia is, as the Bible says, a 'deep sleep' artificially induced. Only God could have done it *then;* and only God could have told Adam how it was done.

Note 3—God's mercy is shown in sparing Adam unnecessary pain, and God's efficiency is shown in His closing up the wound.

Note 4—There is a famous Greek story somewhat on the same lines:

'One day Zeus had a headache. So Hephaestus the fire-god took an axe and chopped open Zeus's head. Out sprang Athena, fully-armed for war!' (Zeus apparently recovered without special treatment).

Compare this absurd legend with the dignified Bible account.

It is not difficult to perceive which is miracle-fiction and which is miracle-*fact*.

Note 5—A man has both X and Y chromosomes
whereas a woman has only X.

So part of a woman's body could never be built-up (by multiplication of cells) into a man's body—the Y chromosomes would be missing.

But part of a man's body *could* be built up into a woman's because he has *everything* she needs for her body.

Once again, the Bible story makes sense according to *science*.

Verse 22.   and brought her to Adam.

Verse 23.   And the man said, This is now bone of my bones, and flesh of my flesh; she shall be called Woman, because she was taken out of Man.

Note 1—*Why* did God choose this extraordinary method of creating the first humans?

Answer—a—To show that man's relationship with his wife is far closer than any animal's with its mate.

When Adam later studied the animals he would have found that though some (e.g. pigeons) mate for life, most are promiscuous (i.e. have several mates).

He might have thought that humans too could have several mates (at least in the *next* generation).

But by creating Woman in this special way, God taught Adam that His plan is *one* man with *one* woman for *life*.

Verses 21, 22, 23, 24 and 25

b—To teach us that as the whole human race came from *one man,* Adam, so for the whole human race there is only *one Saviour,* Christ. St. Paul explains this in Romans 5 and I Corinthians 15.

Verse 24. **Therefore shall a man leave his father and his mother and shall be joined to his wife:**
and they shall be one flesh.

Note 1—Jesus said these words were spoken by God (Mat.19.4).
Because of the special way in which Eve was created, God has made a special law for *every* husband in *every* land in *every* age:

MARRIAGE IS THE *SUPREMELY IMPORTANT* RELATIONSHIP.

Note 2—How very extraordinary this law seems to be.
A man owes his life and existence to his father and mother, yet in some mysterious way he is *more closely related* to his wife than to his parents!

Note 3—No man would have dared to make this law, because it is so *unpopular.*
Henry VIII with his six wives was no freak:
in all ages men have wanted sexual freedom.
Henry VIII would have liked to wipe this verse out of the Bible but he dared not: he knew it was the command of GOD.

Note 4—Many religions teach that grown-up children should look after their parents,
but *only* the Bible says that a man should put his wife *first.*

Note 5—Experience down the ages has proved that the Bible is right.
In some countries, mothers-in-law rule the roost and make life a misery for their daughters-in-law.
The Chinese symbol for 'trouble' shows two women under one roof!
Most couples are happier living away from parents.
You can still *honour* them by keeping in touch and supporting them financially, if necessary.

Verse 25. **And they were both naked, Adam and his wife, and were not ashamed.**

Note 1—Why? does this mean the Nudists are right?

Answer—No! the Nudists are not right.
Adam and Eve (we get her name from 3.20) wore no clothes because
a—the climate was sub-tropical, so they needed no warmth.
Science confirms that dense vegetation once covered the globe.
b—all earth's plants and creatures were harmless (no thorns or thistles, leeches or mosquitos), so they needed no protection.
c—they had no shame because they had never *sinned.*

Note 2—Sex is a gift of God and in itself absolutely pure, nothing to be 'ashamed of'.

But *we* are *not* as Adam and Eve were before they sinned.

We are sin-ful people, and our thoughts and imagination naturally go the *wrong* way.

Note 3—Animals have no shame because they had no Fall (into sin).

We are not shame-less animals, but humans to whom shame is a God-given instinct.

We know this because after Adam and Eve had tried to clothe themselves (3.7), God gave them better clothes (3.21).

Note 4—Nudists are trying to make a Paradise on Earth, which God has said is *impossible* until Christ returns to change everything. (Philippians 3.21).

WHAT DID EVE LOOK LIKE?

We are not told, but John Milton in his famous poem 'Paradise Lost' calls her 'fairest of her daughters, Eve'.

This is not hard to believe, because as the crown of God's creation she must have been very beautiful.

Was she blonde or brunette?

The question is a valid one because (as St Paul tells us in I Cor.11) a woman's long hair is her glory, she may well be proud of it.

Have you ever thought of this fact:

Man is the only primate whose head-hair never stops growing? (an Indian priest holds the record—26 feet! (GBR)).

Evolution-artists' pictures of ape-*men* are bad enough, but when they come to ape-*women* the effect is really frightful: flat-breasted, snub-nosed, wide-mouthed, short-haired, unkempt, and of course always *dark*. No blondes! No Swedish beauties!—because these would look far too feminine and human-like.

Remember (it needs to be repeated)—
these ape-men/ape-women pictures are pure fantasy and fiction.

No bones of any shape or size can tell us the length or colour of the owner's hair, or the shape of her bust or nose.

Now it is our turn to ask the Evolutionist

SOME MORE QUESTIONS

1—Why did one group of ape-like creatures (our 'common ancestor') *keep* their useful protective body-hair, which never needs cutting, while evolving into apes;

whereas another group of the same creatures (again, the 'common ancestor')

Eve

lost nearly all their useful protective body-hair, and acquired long useless head-hair, which often needs cutting, while evolving into humans?

2—Which came first—long head-hair, or cutting tools?

Because TOE has never answered these questions, Evolution-artists are really puzzled to know how to draw an ape-woman.

If they give her a crew-cut, she will look too ape-like;

if they give her long hair, she will look too woman-like;

so they usually compromise on the bobbed style of the 1920s!

In fact, only

THE BIBLE ANSWER MAKES SENSE

Note 1—Apes and monkeys were provided with short body-hair which does *not* need cutting, because God knew

    a—they could never make or use tools,

    b—long head-hair would be a distinct *dis*-advantage in the jungle,

    c—they would never have the skill to make clothes,

    d—their babies have to cling to mother's hair in the tree-tops.

Note 2—Eve was created with long and ever-growing hair as the crown of her beauty.

She was not designed for jungle-living, and in any case her hands soon learned the art of hair-*dressing*.

Note 3—Adam's hair, too, kept growing; but he was given the wisdom to make tools to cut it, as 'nature itself' taught him (I Cor.11.14).

Note 4—God knew that Adam and Eve would be able to make themselves clothes instead of body-hair.

Conclusion: Throw away all the drawings of ape-women, and picture to yourself the fairest 'Miss Universe' imaginable.

You may then get somewhere near the truth of real, beautiful Eve.

Chimpanzee mother

GENESIS CHAPTER THREE

Paradise Lost — Physical effects of the Curse — Cave men and 'civil' men.

Note—the main purpose of this book is to compare Scripture with Science, so in the remaining chapters we shall comment only on those verses which *appear* to be scientifically 'incorrect'.

Verse 1. Now the serpent was more subtle (crafty or clever) than any beast of the field which the Lord God had made.

Note 1—Probably the most important word in this statement is 'was'.

Moses is not stating a fact of nature as he *observed* it in 1400 B.C. but a *revealed* fact of nature as it was in the dawn of history. It is very likely that God's curse upon the serpent reduced its 'brain-power'.

Note 2—Though the snake is now far less 'intelligent' than the elephant, dolphin, chimpanzee and dog, he is still the Artful Dodger of the animal world.

When Jesus told His disciples to be 'wise as serpents', He probably meant 'clever at keeping out of trouble'. This is the reputation which snakes still have in countries where they are plentiful.

Snakes also have a transparent cap over their eyes, instead of eyelids, so it is difficult to tell whether they are asleep—or watching you.

1(b): and he said unto the woman . . .

CAN SNAKES TALK?

Note 1—The only answer Science can give is: we don't know of any talking snakes *today*.

Note 2—In the story of Balaam (Numbers 22.28) God enabled a donkey to speak, and the Apostle Peter assures us that this really happened (II Peter 2.16)—a *divine* miracle.

Note 3—Revelation 12.9 calls the Devil 'that old serpent, Satan, the deceiver'. So it seems that this was a devilish *(diabolical)* miracle. Satan somehow entered into the serpent, just as the demons in the Gospel story entered into the pigs (Mark 5).

Note 4—By nature a snake's tongue is not now adapted for speech; but it once may have been, just as parrots and mynahs can learn to talk—although their tongues were obviously not *made* for this.

PHYSICAL CHANGES BROUGHT ON BY ADAM'S SIN

Verse 14.   And the Lord God said unto the serpent, Because you have done this, cursed are you above (more than) all cattle, and above (more than) all wild animals;

Note 1—This seems to imply that all animals have to some extent come under the curse of God.

We see this in

a—animal diseases, which are numerous.

Dogs get distemper and rabies; horses get sleeping-sickness; cows catch tuberculosis; pigs have foot-and-mouth disease, swine-fever etc. None of these things are 'good', so none of them can have been created by God at the beginning.

b—Beasts began to prey on each other only *after* Adam's sin (which is called 'the Fall of Man').

Lions, tigers etc. (and some dinosaurs) now exchanged their vegetarian diet (1.29) for flesh and blood, and all Nature became 'red in tooth and claw'.

Instinctively we feel that this cannot have been God's highest and best will, and we are right. It wasn't.

Nature 'Red in tooth and claw'

WHY SHOULD INNOCENT ANIMALS SUFFER FOR MAN'S SIN?

*Answer—*Jesus taught that God cares for every sparrow, but at the same time He said,

'You (humans) are of more value than many sparrows' (Luke 12).

The death of any animal is 'sad',
but the death of a person's *soul* is a million times more tragic. God's curse fell on innocent animals to remind us humans of the *terrible result of human sin,* and to show us the need for a New Earth and New Heaven where there will be no bloodshed, tears or pain (Revelation 21).

**14(b) upon your belly you shall go,
and dust shall you eat all the days of your life.**

---

*Note 1—*Almost certainly this means that God's curse deprived the snake of legs. Evolutionists agree that snakes once had legs, but according to TOE they lost them—over "millions of years", of course—because in dense vegetation it is easier to move without legs. But the same sentence (EB 1964) admits that the loss of limbs was a degeneration, i.e. becoming worse. This contradicts the whole Theory Evolution, which states that only the stronger, faster, cleverer creatures survived, and that all permanent changes must have been for the *better.* Even now it is obvious that lizards (with legs) can climb trees much faster than snakes without legs. And most snakes do not live in dense vegetation. At every point TOE fails to fit the facts; but the Bible explains them all.

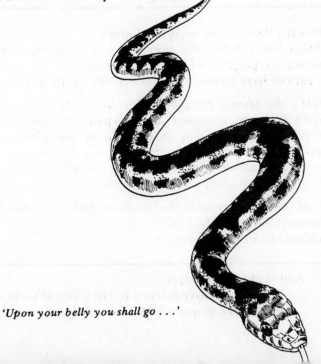

'Upon your belly you shall go . . .'

Note 2—'Eat dust' may be a metaphorical way of saying 'live down in the dust', or it may refer to the snake's use of its *tongue*.

'A snake keeps flicking out its tongue while moving along the ground, because it is the snake's organ of touch. A snake also uses its tongue to pick up particles and put them into two tiny cavities in the roof of its mouth. These cavities are linked with the snake's sense of smell. By picking up the particles, the tongue helps the snake to smell'. (WBE)

While we admire the Creator's wisdom in inventing such a device, we instinctively *despise* a creature which has to put its tongue on the ground in order to feel and smell. This was God's purpose: to remind us, every time we see a snake, that enticing others to sin is *despicable*.

Verse 15. **'And I will put enmity between you and the woman, and between your descendants and her descendants . . .'**

Note 1—This 'enmity' is shown in the instinctive dislike most of us feel towards snakes. Probably it was at this time that God introduced POISON into the fangs of some species; and because we know that *some* snakes can kill, we fear and distrust them all.

Verse 16. **Unto the woman God said:** **'I will greatly multiply your pain in childbearing; in pain you shall bring forth children.'**

Note 1—This is a 'fact of life' everyone knows.

When Mum has a baby, she must go into hospital. She will need doctors, nurses, anaesthesia, possibly a Caesarean operation.

But the cat can have kittens at home any day—with no trouble at all!

Note 2—WHY do female humans suffer so much more than female animals?

Once again TOE has no answer—because pain, obviously, does not help anyone in the 'struggle for survival'. Why should Man, the most 'successful' mammal, have the greatest difficulty in reproducing his species? The only answer that makes sense is the Bible answer: childbirth pains result directly from God's punishment of Eve and hence of all women.

Project: Find out what percentage of mothers died in childbirth
    a—in Europe/USA in the C19th
    b—in Africa/Asia in this century

Verse 17. **And God said to Adam:** **Because you have listened to the voice of your wife, and have eaten of the tree about which I commanded you—'You shall not eat of**

Verses 14, 15, 16, 17, 18 and 19

it'—cursed is the ground because of you; in toil you shall eat of it all the days of your life;

Verse 18. thorns and thistles it shall bring forth to you; and you shall eat the plants of the field.

Verse 19. In the sweat of your face shall you eat bread . . .

Note 1—Evolution has no explanation to offer for the existence of *thorns.* 'They protect the plant', some say.

So roses are protected, and dahlias unprotected.

But over the centuries dahlias have 'survived', apparently, just as well as roses.

Similarly, blackberries and gooseberries have thorns, raspberries and strawberries have none. But all grow equally well—even in the wild.

Once again, *the Bible explanation fits the facts.*

God put thorns onto *some* plants—mercifully, not all—to remind us that this world is under His curse.

Note 2—*Thistles* are mentioned perhaps because they are the most *obviously* unpleasant and useless of weeds. Also (like thorns) they are common in nearly every part of the world—and God intended the Bible for the whole world.

WBE carries separate articles on fifty different kinds of weed, and informs us that they cost the USA about £2000,000,000 a year.

Note 3—Besides thistles and thorns, many other things combine to make life tough for the farmer in most countries:

a—*Insects:* less than 1% of the 800,000 species are harmful, but these few thousand do a powerful lot of damage—estimated at £3000 million a year in the USA alone.

Thorns and thistles

67

Locusts

In Africa and Asia locusts are appallingly destructive. Hundreds of millions fly in one swarm, and in one day they can eat as much as four million elephants can (Guinness Book of Records).

b—*Drought* causes terrible hardship in some part of the world almost every year. Nine million died in the 1877—79 famine in China.

'Drought-stricken Australia has experimented for years with seeding clouds with silver iodide crystals to persuade the moisture it is time to precipitate (fall), but success has only been moderate and the climate has been scarcely disturbed by the scientific rainmakers.' (Daily Telegraph report, 14 July 1975)

c—*Blight* destroyed the potato crop in Ireland 1845—47, and 750,000 (out of 8 million) died of starvation.

Note 4—Even under ideal conditions in a temperate climate, farming is *hard labour*—ploughing, sowing, reaping, threshing, storing.

Very different from the light garden work originally given to Adam.

Note 5—Even after the grain has been successfully harvested it must be ground, sifted, mixed with water, kneaded and baked, before it can be eaten. 'What a sweat!'—compared with plucking fruit off a tree.

Note 6—God's curse upon the earth includes everything that we (rightly) call 'bad' weather and natural disasters: storms, floods, tornados, earthquakes etc. In Britain these are so rare that we forget how frequent and destructive they are in other parts of the world.

'About 50,000 earthquakes occur *every year* over the whole earth. Of these about 100 are large enough to produce substantial destruction . . . the very great earthquakes occur at an average rate of about one per year' (EB). 1974's in Pakistan killed 5300 people, 1970's in Peru killed 47,194.

Similarly *hurricanes* rip through the Western hemisphere at least once every two years. In September 1974 Hurricane Fifi killed 7500—8000 people and left more than 300,000 homeless in Honduras. 'There is no agreement among scientists about how a hurricane actually starts. If there were, the information would have been used to nip baby hurricanes in the bud' (D.T. as above).

So—earth is *no longer* 'very good', no longer a Paradise.

It will remain 'this present evil world' (Galatians 1.4) until the Return of Christ.

WHAT ABOUT STONE AGE MAN?

'Prehistory' textbooks often state that man was first a hunter, then a farmer.

The Bible, on the other hand, states that Adam became a farmer immediately after he was turned out of Eden ('**the Lord God sent him forth from the garden to till the ground** . . . 3.23).

Which account is true?

Note 1—All historical records of the oldest civilizations show man as a farmer from the beginning—e.g. in Egypt, Babylon, India, China etc.

Of course this does not mean they did *not* hunt, but they did not *depend* on hunting, and they did know how to raise crops.

Note 2—The dates given for pre-historic man (e.g. Neanderthal and Cro-Magnon) cannot be proved and are very probably wrong.

All chemical dating methods depend on *assumptions* (taking something for granted), and most scientists take it for granted that earth's atmosphere has always been much the same as it is today.

But other scientists think that before the Flood our atmosphere was very different, with a 'water canopy' shielding the earth from harmful cosmic rays. This would change the estimated age of fossils from hundreds of thousands to just a few thousand years.[26/27]

Note 3—Dating rocks by Uranium and Potassium-Argon has been proved to be totally unreliable. 'Lava rocks known to have been formed in 1800/1801 in Hulalai, Hawaii, show an age of 160 million years by the Potassium-Argon method. Another report in "Science" for October 11, 1968, shows dates of 12 to 21 million years for volcanic rocks known to be less than 200 years old'.[3, 7]

Note 4—It seems probable that 'cave-men' have existed *alongside* 'civilized' man from earliest times.

(2000 B.C.) Job 24 speaks of men who '**seek diligently for prey (i.e. hunt) in the wilderness**'
and '**are wet with the showers of the mountains,
and embrace the rock for want of shelter** . . .
**in the clefts of the valleys must they dwell,
in holes of the earth and of the rocks**' (Job 30).

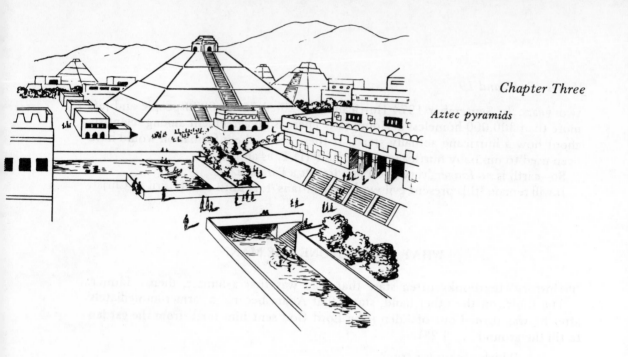

Herodotus, the 'Father of History', writes of the Thracians (northern Greece) in 500 B.C.:

'They consider the *agricultural labourer* of all men the *least worthy* of respect. The best sources of income are war and plunder'!

Needless to say, these Thracians produced no architecture, no sculpture, no literature, no drama, no music, mathematics or philosophy—although they lived only a few hundred miles from the Athenians' culture and civilization.

Note 5—Cave-dwellers exist today in New Mexico and the Philippines.

Some African tribes live only by hunting, and herding cattle. But no one doubts that they are related to other tribes who are farmers.

Note 6—Many South American tribes who now live in primitive huts in the jungle, eating wild manioc, fish and monkeys, are descendants of the Mayas, Aztecs and Incas, who were expert builders, astronomers, craftsmen, warriors and farmers.

They even knew how to dehydrate potatoes.

This proves that there is no 'law' of man evolving upward from barbarism. Sometimes it is the other way round: man *devolves* or *degenerates* from 'civil' man to cave-man, from farmer to hunter.

And this, we believe, is what happened to Adam's descendants: some got lost in the caves and forests, while others *at the same time* were developing the skills which built the Ark, the Great Pyramid, and Stonehenge.

SUMMING UP

Note 1—There is no truly scientific proof that any man (or animal) lived hundreds of thousands of years ago.

Verses 17, 18 and 19

Note 2—'Stone Age Man', the hunter, probably lived at the same time as civilized man, the farmer, throughout ancient history. Even in one family—Isaac's—one son (Esau) was a hunter, the other (Jacob) a shepherd: 1700 B.C.

Note 3—Written *records* remain only of civilized man, of course, because the jungle/cave men lost the art of writing. (See Genesis 5 and 11, notes).

Note 4—We know almost nothing about man's development before the Flood (i.e. before about 3000 B.C.), which must have wiped out nearly all trace of the first two thousand years of Man's history.

Note 5—Bearing this in mind, we have no reason to doubt the Bible statement that Earliest Man was a farmer.

GENESIS CHAPTER FOUR

'Stone age' : B.C. and A.D. — Cain's wife.

Verse 17.   . . . Cain's wife conceived and bore Enoch.

Note 1—'Where did Cain get his wife?' has been a stock question for centuries, but the answer is quite simple:

she was one of his sisters.

Nowadays we regard it as genetically unwise to marry a sister, and the Law of Moses forbids it (Leviticus 18).

But when God planned to start the human race from one pair, He must have foreseen that this would happen—at least in the first generation. Daughters are not mentioned till 5.4; but it is probable that Cain was married at the time he murdered Abel, and took his wife with him into banishment.

Verse 19.   And Lamech took unto him two wives . . .

Note 1—Evolutionists tell us that man was at first 'promiscuous' like the monkeys, living in troops with all females common. Then little by little (they say) it became a tribal 'custom' for each male to mate with one female only.

What is the evidence for this theory? There is *none*!

In fact, marriage customs vary enormously all over the world (see the article on 'Marriage' in EB).

Some tribes (but few) have women in common; others have very strict rules for monogamy (one-man-one-wife) and severe punishments for adultery.

The Bible account fits the facts very well. God's original plan was one man + one woman for life, but soon bad men like Lamech began to despise God's arrangement and to grab an extra wife or two.

Verse 21.   Jubal was the father of all such as handle the harp and pipe (i.e. string and wind instruments) . . .

Verse 22.   Tubal-cain, the forger (maker) of every cutting instrument of brass (or copper) and iron.

Verses 17, 19, 21 and 22

Note 1—These words give a hint of man's remarkable progress in Art and Craft in the pre-Flood civilization.

Note 2—One of the many questions that Evolution has failed to answer is:

'Since man became "homo sapiens" at least 50,000 years ago—according to your theory—why did he not invent things (buildings, tools, ships, writing, agriculture, muscial instruments) scores of thousands of years ago, instead of only a few thousand?'

(We know from the size of their skulls that Neanderthal and Cro-Magnon men were at least as intelligent as ourselves).

Once again *the Bible is our true guide to anthropology:* some races (or tribes) have always been cleverer than others at inventing things.

There is no reason why 'Stone Age Man' should not have lived in Europe or Turkey *at the same time* as men like Jubal and Tubal-cain lived in the Middle East. Until very recently, Australian aborigines were using more than fifty kinds of *stone tools*—for carpentry, hunting, fighting, fishing, cooking etc.—although the Stone Age is supposed to have ended around 3000 B.C.

And remember, there is no scientifically-proven reliable method of dating flint arrowheads etc.[7, 9]

Stone tools

GENESIS CHAPTER FIVE

'Camp-fire-story' myth — Ages extra-ordinary, not incredible — remarkable coincidence.

Verse 1. This is the book of the generations of Adam.

Note 1— Notice the word *book*.

Professor R. K. Harrison, of Toronto University, comments:

'the specific usage of "sepher" (Hebrew for 'book') is to be understood strictly in terms of a *written document*'. (Introduction to the OT p.535).

CAMP FIRE STORY?

For many years a strange MYTH has been floating round RE classrooms—we may call it the 'Camp-Fire-Story Myth'.

RE textbooks picture Bedouin greybeards in the flickering firelight telling 'Tales of a Grandfather' to eager children with popping eyes. *This,* we are told, is the way the Bible came to us . . . hundreds of years of story-telling (which includes, of course, quite a bit of exaggeration and legend); then the stories written down by some brilliant (but unknown) scribes; and finally, the various strands woven together by an even more brilliant (but still unknown) 'editor', to make the Book of Genesis![54]

For this 'artistic reconstruction' of history there is no real evidence whatever. It is a fantasy based on the mischievous and mistaken Theory of Evolution, which includes the idea that Early Man could not *write.* Now let us examine the facts:

*Note 2—*Genesis 5 could never have come in a 'Told To The Children' series because it is *not a story*. It could never have survived except as a *written record,* which is implied by the word 'book' in v.1. (Sagas like Homer's Odyssey might have been memorised for years before they were written down, because they are *poetry*.

But who would care to memorise Genesis 5?)

*Note 3—*An astonishing feature of ancient civilizations is their grasp of *astronomy*. And astronomy depends on written records.

For instance, Thales (p.19) could not have predicted the eclipse in 585 B.C. unless he knew of previous eclipses recorded at intervals of 18 years and 11 days.

Verse 1

It is almost certain that records like this were kept by the Egyptians (on papyrus) and by the Babylonians (on clay tablets) 2000 years before Thales, because they knew the length of a solar year, and much more, at the time the Great Pyramid was built.

Note 4—Wherever we find civilized man, there we find writing—as early as 3000 B.C. in Sumeria (Iraq).[55]

So there is no reason to doubt that Adam from the beginning kept a record of passing days and years—since God had given him the sun and the stars for this purpose (1.14).

Note 5—Adam's godly descendants carried on the records; Noah took these into the Ark; and finally this genealogy/chronology was included by Moses in the story of Israel's beginnings.

This interpretation makes sense and fits in perfectly with the very precise noting of every important birth marriage and death, which we find in the later chapters of Genesis.

Note 6—Edwin Yamauchi in his book 'The Stones and the Scriptures' (1973) shows that not more than *one in a million* ancient documents have been brought to light by archaeology (e.g. out of 112 million Roman Army pay vouchers issued A.D.1—300, only six and a half have been found).[37]

The Mangyan tribe in the Philippines use *wood* to carve their peculiar script on, and the ancient Tamils of South India used *leaves* to write their history, so very few 'originals' have survived.

Perhaps Adam and the antediluvians (men before the Flood) used similar materials. So our Scriptures are copies of copies of copies . . . but there is good reason to believe that the original *written records* go right back to the dawn of History.

Project: What is the first birthday celebration mentioned in the Bible?

Find out
1—the approximate date and the full name of the person concerned.
2—how that civilization kept annual records.

Clue: the story of Joseph.

Egyptian pyramids

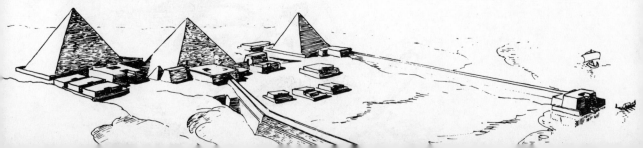

Verse 5.   So all the days that Adam lived were 930 years; and he died.

Note 1—Can we believe these ages?

Answer—If, as many scientists believe, there was a water-canopy all round the globe before the Flood, this would have protected all living things from the harmful cosmic rays which tend to shorten life. Man would then have lived longer, and animals would have grown bigger.

This is confirmed by the discovery of hundreds of 'giant' fossils, e.g. turtles 10 foot long, dragon-flies with a two-foot wing span, the 51 foot Texan pterodactyl etc. Crocodiles grew to over 50 feet, about three times as long as modern ones.

Now, since growth is always in three dimensions, this means that prehistoric crocodiles weighed *27 times* as much as modern ones, and must have lived many times longer in order to grow to such a size. So it is not hard to believe that 'prehistoric' (which really means pre-Flood) man could have lived to ten or twelve times the modern average of 70 years.

a—The Jewish historian Josephus (100 A.D.) writes that 12 ancient historians of other nations agree with the Bible that men before the Flood lived to nearly 1000 years. (Antiquities Book I. ch.3 section 9).

b—Where the book of Genesis can be checked (e.g. in Egyptian customs and names) it has been proved to be extraordinarily accurate.

So it is reasonable to believe that it is equally accurate in statements which can*not* be checked.

Giant prehistoric turtle

c—'Recent research makes it clear that the *truly primitive peoples of the world must have been far healthier* than most of today's world . . . civilization dealt a blow to man's health from which he is only now recovering.' Daily Telegraph magazine, July 1975.

Note 2—The purpose of this chapter is *both* to give a chronology of the time from Adam to the Flood (1656 years)
and to show that God has always had some true worshippers ('prophets . . . since the world began' Luke 1.70).

Their lives overlapped by hundreds of years, e.g. Lamech, Noah's father, was 86 when Adam died. So any tradition (or written documents, clay tablets etc.) that Adam wanted to pass on was only in the 2nd generation at the time of the Flood.

Note 3—Most old civilizations had some kind of dating system, and not one of them put the Creation of the World earlier than 7000 B.C.
Here are some typical dates:[56]

Indian	6204 B.C.
Arabian	6174
Babylonian	6158
Chinese	6157
Persian	5507
Abyssinian	5500
(Central American) Mayan	3113

Note 4—Modern archaeological dating is changeable and unreliable. In the 1929 Encyclopaedia Britannica the date of the Great Pyramid was given as 4800 B.C. Ten years later it dropped *a thousand years* to 3800 B.C. Since then it has dropped *another thousand* years to 2850 or 2600 B.C. And in each case it was an 'expert' who made the calculation.

So the age of the Earth, and of Man, may be very much younger than is supposed.

Verse 24.   And Enoch walked with God; and he was not; for God took him.

Q.—What happened?

Answer—Enoch went up to heaven alive, just as Elijah went up alive (II Kings 2), and just as all true Christians

'shall be caught up together . . . in the clouds to meet the Lord in the air' when He returns (I Thes.4).

God, who made the law of gravity, can override His own laws when He chooses— as Jesus did when walking on the sea (Matthew 14).

Verse 31.   and all the days of Lamech were 777 years; and he died.

It is interesting to note that Lamech, Noah's father, died five years before the Flood (5.30 with 7.6); and Methuselah, Noah's grandfather, died in the very year the Flood came, thus:

Lamech lived before Noah's birth	182 years
Noah lived before the Flood	600 years
Total years from Lamech to Flood	782

which is the same figure as Methuselah's years after Lamech's birth (v.26).

It must have been a great relief to Noah *not* having to look after Dad and Grandpa on the Ark in their extreme old age.

GENESIS CHAPTER SIX

> *Giants, ancient and modern — Myth of man's 'essential goodness' — Violence, ancient and modern — Myth of a local flood — Ark seaworthy — Ark's capacity — Miracles of migration — Food stores stupendous.*

Verse 4.   There were giants on the earth in those days.

Were there really?

Note 1—No problem here, if we accept the popular definition of a giant as a person over 7 ft tall.

The Guinness Book of Records lists 8 modern men over 8 ft and many more over 7 ft. In the Anatomical Museum of Birmingham University Medical School stands the skeleton of a 7 ft 9 inch woman who died in 1921.

Note 2—It is a common experience that even a man of 6 ft will feel 'dwarfed' by a man only 20% taller (see Numbers 13.33: '**we became like grasshoppers in our own sight**'). This is because the giant's *total* size will be 2/3 more than his own.

(Weight varies as the cube of height.

   If a man of 70 inches weighs 150 lbs
   then a man of 84 inches will weigh 150 x $\frac{6^3}{5}$ = 260 lbs)

Note 3—No prehistoric giant skeletons have yet been found, but the EB (article 'Dwarfism and Gigantism') admits that humans, like other mammals, probably grew to outsize proportions in those days:

'Large skeletal fragments have been found in Java, and molars of tremendous dimensions were located in China and ascribed by some investigators to a human stock . . . It may not be too far from the truth if we suggest the Java giant was much bigger than any living gorilla and that the Chinese giant was twice as large as a male gorilla'.

Note 4—The ancient Greeks had a strong tradition that Giants lived in the early days of the human race. Fantastic *myths* were woven around them, such as Atlas being compelled to hold up the sky as a punishment for rebellion against Zeus. The Bible has no myths at all, but simply records the fact that there were some extra large people on earth before the Flood.

Verse 5. **The Lord saw that the wickedness of man was great in the earth, and that every imagination of the thoughts of his heart was only evil continually.**

Note 1—In the C19th many people believed that the human race was progressing towards a new era of peace, plenty and prosperity.

There was no problem that Science could not solve!

Then came the Great War of 1914—18.

Dreams were shattered as the most 'advanced' nations of the world fought like savages.

Here was a problem that Science could *not* solve:

the basic wickedness of the human heart.

Note 2—The Bible gives no details of how man's wickedness was shown, except the word **'violence'** (v.11).

We may catch some idea of the truth by looking back to just a few of the violent things that man has done *since* the Flood.

WHY was God **'sorry He had made man'** (v.6)?

a—*Roman Gladiators.* These men (usually slaves) were compelled to fight in pairs until one or the other was killed. Scores of thousands of men and women sat enjoying the spectacle. In 45 B.C. Julius Caesar gave a 'free show' of 300 gladiator fights. A later Emperor, Titus (who destroyed Jerusalem and crucified 100,000 Jews outside the city) ordered a show lasting 100 days. Yet another, Trajan (A.D.107) exhibited 5000 pairs of gladiators and the slaughter of 11,000 animals. Every large town throughout the Roman Empire had its arena and annual 'games' (= killings). One historian has calculated that 'the combats of the amphitheatre cost from 20,000 to 30,000 lives *per month* . . . no war ever waged has caused so much slaughter as these "games"!' (They were finally abolished by a *Christian* Emperor).

b—War has always been frightful, but we may be thankful we do not live in the days of the *Mongols.*

'It was a Mongol custom to cut off an ear from each corpse of their massacred foes, and on this occasion (Poland, A.D.1242) they filled nine sacks with these ghastly trophies . . .' 'the inhabitants were slaughtered without regard to age or sex . . . impaled, flayed, roasted alive . . .' (Bulgaria, A.D.1237).

'On the 15th of February 1263 the Mongols sacked Baghdad . . . for seven days it was given up to pillage, fire and sword. The number of killed is said to have reached 800,000' (four times as many as were killed by the atom bomb on Hiroshima).

c—The *Aztecs* of Mexico (A.D.1500) had some rather unsavoury customs.

'In front of the altar of the war-god stood the green stone of sacrifice, humped so as to bend upward the body of the victim in order that the priest might more easily slash open the breast with his obsidian (stone) knife, tear out the heart and hold it up before the god, while the captor and his friends were waiting below for the carcase to be tumbled down the steps for them to carry home to be cooked for the feast of victory.

From the terrace could be seen 70 or more other temples . . . with their images and blazing fires, and the "skull-place" where the skulls of victims by tens of thousands were skewered on cross-sticks or built into towers . . .' (EB)

Similar examples of horrible cruelty could be found in the history of almost every country (including our own) at some time or other; and of every century (including our own) in some country or other.

Probably the world's violence before the Flood was as bad or worse, because man left to himself (i.e. without the Gospel of Christ) is naturally cruel.

THE IMPORTANCE OF THE FLOOD

We may judge this by a comparison with English history.

If someone were to write a book of 900 pages covering the period from William the Conqueror to 1975 (i.e. roughly one year to a page, on average), and were to give *112 pages* to describing the events of *one* year (say 1940), you might guess that he thought those events to be *very important* indeed.

This is about the same proportion that the writer of Genesis has given to Noah's Flood. The whole book covers 2300 years, but 1/20th of the book is given to the story of *one* year, the Year of the Flood. This shows that the writer considers the Flood to be very important indeed.

DID IT REALLY HAPPEN?

Let's think for a moment: how do we know *anything* happened—in the days before photography and TV?

For example, the assassination of Julius Caesar on 13 March 44 B.C.

No one living today has seen Caesar's bones or the weapons that killed him.

No one has a tape-recording of his words, 'You too, Brutus!'

But most people believe it happened, because Will Shakespeare wrote a play about it.

Shakespeare got his information from a Greek historian named Plutarch who wrote in the first century A.D.

So we believe a 2000-year-old story about a Roman because 400 years ago an Englishman wrote a play based upon a Greek biography written by a man who was born 90 years after Caesar is said to have died!

Now—what about the Flood?

The evidence that it really happened is very much stronger than the evidence for Caesar's assassination. It might well be said that it is *stronger than the evidence for any event of Ancient History* before Christ.

WORLD-WIDE TRADITIONS

Stories of a gigantic flood that destroyed nearly all mankind are found all over the globe. The most detailed accounts come, as we would expect, from countries nearest to Ararat, where the Ark landed (ch.8.4). Other versions turn up in Persia, India, Burma, Indonesia, Sarawak, New Guinea, Tahiti, Hawaii, China, Japan, Siberia, Australia (among the aborigines) and New Zealand (Maoris), Alaska (Eskimos), North America (Red Indians), South America, Egypt, Sudan, Nigeria, Congo, South Africa, Greece, Iceland, Lithuania, Finland, Lapland, Wales and Ireland.[32] (This agrees with 9.19: **'From these three sons of Noah the whole earth is populated'**).

Of course *now* the Bible has come to all these countries, but the Flood 'legends' were independent of the Bible, passed down over the centuries in scores of tribal languages.

Some details are specially interesting:

1—Ixtlilxochitl, the native historian of the Aztecs, says that the first world lasted 1716 years before it was destroyed by a flood.

(This figure is only 60 years different from the 1656 years which the Bible gives us—by addition of the ages in Genesis 5).

2—The Chinese character (symbol) for a large ship is a combination of the figure 8 and the symbol for 'mouths' or 'persons'.

(Noah + Shem, Ham, Japheth, + their wives = 8).

3—The Hottentots of South Africa believe they are descended from 'Noh', and the Hawaians report a flood from which only 'Nu-u' and his family were saved.

4—The Greeks still call themselves *Hellenes* from their legendary ancestor Hellen, son of Deucalion. Deucalion and his wife Pyrrha took refuge in a ship loaded with provisions when Zeus decided to destroy the human race by a flood. A Roman poet (B.C.5) describes it thus:

'Sea and land have no distinctions. All is sea, but a sea without a shore. Here one man seeks a hill-top in his flight . . . another catches fish trapped in the elm-trees top . . . the wolf swims among the sheep, lions and tigers are borne along by the waves . . . Most living things are drowned outright.'

We shall note other evidences that the Flood really happened as we go through chapters 7 and 8.

Verse 3. Then the Lord said, 'My spirit shall not strive with man for ever, for he is flesh, but his days shall be 120 years'.

Note 1—This means that God warned everybody, probably through Noah's preaching, that He would judge (punish) the world after 120 years, if people refused to change their ways.

Verses 5, 3, 7 and 13

Note 2—We go back here to answer the question:

WHY DID GOD USE A *FLOOD* TO PUNISH MANKIND?

Why didn't He send an epidemic disease, as He did on the Assyrian army in B.C.710? (II Kings 19.35).

It would have saved Noah a vast amount of time and trouble!

Answer—Probably there were two main reasons:

a—God always gives *warnings* well ahead of time, because He 'hates nothing that He has made', and He wants people to be *saved*. Noah building the Ark on dry land must have been one of the Wonders of the World in those days . . . as the years went by, probably the whole world would have heard about this stupendous project.

So, when the Flood came *they had no excuse.*

b—God intended that throughout the remaining years of man's history the face of the earth should carry awful scars as a reminder to man of the terrible penalty for sin.

Fossils are these 'scars': millions of dead animals, drowned, smothered, mangled, smashed to pieces in a thousand fossil graveyards.

Their message is:

'The wages of sin is *DEATH*!'

Verse 7.   And the Lord said, 'I will blot out man whom I have created from off the face of the ground, man and beast and creeping things and birds of the air, for I am sorry that I have made them'.

Verse 13.   And God said to Noah, '. . . I am about to destroy them *with the earth.'*

Note 1—Some people think the Flood was only local, in the Middle East, not world-wide. However, the last words show that God intended to wipe the *whole* slate clean, as it were.

This agrees with St Peter's statement that 'the world that then existed was deluged with water and perished' (II Peter 3.6).

Note 2—Human fossils have been discovered in China, Java, Africa and North America. This probably indicates that mankind had spread to these countries before the Flood. So in order to drown all humans the waters must have covered *the whole world!*

Note 3—Not only men and animals but also millions of tons of vegetation were destroyed and formed into *coal* by the terrific pressure and heat generated at the time of the Flood.

Until recently, scientists used to think that coal must have taken 'millions of years' to form. But in 1972 Dr Hill of Utah proved by laboratory experiments that coal can be formed from wood *in a very short time*. So most probably the great coal beds were laid down during the year of Noah's Flood.[3]

Verse 14.   'Make yourself an ark of gopher wood . . .'

Note 1—No one knows what wood this was, but cypress seems the most likely. Alexander the Great used it to build a fleet, and the cypress doors of St Peter's Cathedral, Rome, have remained undecayed for upwards of 1000 years.[57]

Note 2—The Ark (see diagram) was a perfectly reasonable shape, not unlike a modern barge—built more to float than to sail.

The 'Great Britain' designed by Brunel in 1844 had dimensions of 322 ft by 51 by 32½, almost exactly the same proportions as the Ark (length ten times the height, six times the width). Brunel had 1000 years of British shipbuilding experience to draw on, but the Ark was the first of its kind.

Note 3—The Babylonians too had a flood-story. But they made the Ark a CUBE 180 ft long 180 wide and 180 high . . . not very seaworthy.

This is an excellent illustration of the difference between *legends* and *history*. The Babylonian story is obviously a legend, passed down from generation to generation by word of mouth, and therefore inaccurate in several details. (It is much easier to tell your grandchildren about a *cubic* ship, because you need to remember only one figure!)

On the other hand the Ark's true dimensions must have been *written down* at the time of Noah, and so became a part of real *history*. It is most unlikely that the Hebrews, who were not a sea-going people, would have correctly guessed figures which agree so well with the dimensions used by experienced shipbuilders.

Note 4—Q.—Could Noah and Sons have built such an enormous vessel?

It had a displacement tonnage of nearly 20,000 tons, and was the largest ship ever built until the Cunard liner ETURIA in 1884.[1]

Answer—a—Probably Noah used the help of hired men.

He may have had scores of servants, as Job had (Job 1.3).

b—Oddly enough, ancient civilizations specialised in building on a colossal scale after the Flood. The Great Pyramid of Gizeh, Egypt, is constructed of more than two million enormous blocks of limestone each weighing 2½ tons. Its four sides, each of them twice the length of a football field, are set to the points of the compass to an accuracy of an eleventh of one degree. Stonehenge (perhaps 1800 B.C.) is another marvel, with 50-ton blocks aligned to mark the winter and summers solstices. Many other structures from Iran to Ireland (not forgetting Easter Island) prove that Early Man was an astonishingly capable geometrician and engineer. So Noah was no freak.[40]

Verse 19.   '. . . And of every living thing of all flesh, you shall bring two of every kind into the ark, to keep them alive with you; they shall be male and female.'

BIBLIOGRAPHY

1. The Genesis Flood: Henry Morris and John Whitcomb *(Evangelical Press)*.
2. The Early Earth: J. C. Whitcomb *(Evangelical Press)*.
3. The World That Perished:* J. C. Whitcomb *(Evangelical Press)*.
4. Exposition of Genesis: H. C. Leupold *(Evangelical Press)*.
5. Origin of the Solar System: J. C. Whitcomb *(Presbyterian & Reformed Publishing Co.)*.
6. Why not Creation? edited by Walter Lammerts *(Presbyterian & Reformed Publishing Co.)*.
7. Scientific Studies in Special Creation: edited by Walter Lammerts *(Presbyterian & Reformed Publishing Co.)*.
8. The Creation of Life: A. E. Wilder Smith *(Harold Shaw,* Wheaton, Illinois).
9. Man's Origin, Man's Destiny: A. E. Wilder Smith *(Harold Shaw,* Wheaton, Illinois).
10. After its Kind: Byron Nelson *(Bethany Fellowship Inc.)* (available from C.L.C.).
11. The Wonders of Creation:* Alfred M. Rehwinkel* *(Bethany Fellowship Inc.)* (available from C.L.C.).
12. The Deluge Story in Stone: Byron Nelson *(Bethany Fellowship Inc.)* (available from C.L.C.).
13. Earth's Most Challenging Mysteries: Reginald Daly *(Craig Press)*.
14. Many Infallible Proofs: H. M. Morris *(Creation-Life Publishers)*.
15. Evolution – the Fossils say No! D. T. Gish *(Creation-Life Publishers)*.
16. Scientific Creationism: H. M. Morris *(Creation-Life Publishers)*.
17. Biology: A Search for Order in Complexity:* Creation Research Society *(Zondervan)*.
18. Physical Science for Christian Schools:* E. L. Williams and G. Mulfinger *(Bob Jones University Press)*.
19. Darwin, Evolution, and Creation: P. A. Zimmerman *(Concordia)*.
20. Fossil Man: F. W. Cousins *(Evolution Protest Movement)*.
21. Pamphlet No.160 The Flood: J. E. Shelley *(Evolution Protest Movement)*.
22. Men of Destiny: P. M. Masters *(Evangelical Times)*.
23. Men of Purpose: P. M. Masters *(H. E. Walter Ltd.)*.
24. The Great Brain Robbery: D. C. C. Watson *(H. E. Walter Ltd.)*.
25. Life of J. Clerk Maxwell: Dwight Watson *(Campbell & Garnett)*.
26. a. Monkeys and Typewriters   A. J. Monty White *(privately printed)*.
    b. Radio-Carbon Dating
27. Potassium-Argon Dating: A. J. Monty White *(privately printed)*

28. On the Track of Unknown Animals: B. Heuvelmans *(Paladin)*.
29. The Piltdown Man: R. Millar *(Paladin)*.
30. Fossil Man: M. H. Day *(Hamlyn)*.
31. Modern Man Looks at Evolution: W. W. Fletcher *(Fontana)*.
32. The Flood Reconsidered: F. A. Filby *(Pickering & Inglis)*.
33. Science of Today and Problems of Genesis: P. O'Connell *(Christian Book Club of America,* Hawthorne, California).
34. 'Peking Man': P. O'Connell in Bible-Science Newsletter, July 1969.
35. Fossil Man: R. D. Shaw in Creation Research Society Quarterly, March 1970.
36. Genes, Genesis and Evolution: J. Klotz *(Concordia)*.
37. The Stones and the Scriptures: E. Yamauchi *(IVP)*.
38. Mysterious Universe: Sir James Jeans *(CUP)*.
39. Evolution or Creation? H. Enoch *(Evangelical Press)*.
40. Megalithic Sites in Britain: A. Thom *(OUP)*.
41. Have You Been Brainwashed? D. T. Gish *(Life Messengers booklet)*.
42. Dust or Destiny? *(Fact and Faith)*.
43. Experiences with an Eel *(Fact and Faith)*.
44. Glass Eyes that See *(Fact and Faith)*.
45. God of Creation *(Fact and Faith)*.
46. City of the Bees *(Fact and Faith)*.
47. Red River of Life *(Fact and Faith)*.
48. Darwin and the Beagle: A. Moorehead *(Hamish Hamilton)*.
49. CRSQ December 1974.
50. Herodotus: Histories *(Penguin Classics)*.
51. Piltdown Man, Java Man, Peking Man (tape: *EPM*).
52. Guinness Book of Records.
53. Introduction to the Old Testament: R. K. Harrison *(Tyndale)*.
54. Winding Quest: A. T. Dale *(OUP)*.
55. New Discoveries in Babylonia: P. J. Wiseman *(Marshall Morgan & Scott)*.
56. Young's Analytical Concordance.
57. Jamieson Fausset and Brown: Commentary on the Bible.
58. Customs Culture and Christianity: E. A. Nida *(Tyndale)*.
59. Darwin Retried: Norman Macbeth *(Dell Publishing Co.)*.
60. The Noah's Ark Expedition: F. Navarra *(Coverdale House)*.
61. Radiometric Dating Methods: D. B. Gower *(EPM)*.

* Specially recommended for Teachers in Secondary Schools.

Note—Most of the American books can be obtained from SEND THE LIGHT Trust.

Introducing . . .

CREATION SCIENCE FOUNDATION LTD

A UNIQUE MINISTRY organization promoting the literal accuracy of the Bible as the Word of God, especially as it relates to origins and the Book of Genesis. Creation Science Foundation tells people about the amazing evidence that the universe, the earth within it and life upon it were created — they did not 'evolve' by chance. This evidence for creation, and for the Creator Jesus Christ, is presented in many ways.

* **CREATION** magazine. A unique publication that answers your questions on why you can trust the biblical account of Creation. Easy to read, it will keep you up to date on evidence for God's Creation and Noah's Flood. *Creation* magazine helps you counteract evolution's damaging influences, and shows you the relevance of creation to your daily life. *Creation* magazine has avid readers in more than 40 countries. Ask for a year's subscription and we'll bill you when we send your first issue.

* **BOOKS, TAPES, VIDEOS, FILMS.** Whether layman or scientist you'll find a treasure trove of exciting information in this extensive reading and viewing range. From kindergarten to university academic, creation teaching materials will cater to your need. For leisure reading at home, or for in-depth study, creation science resources will inform and educate you. Ask for catalogues.

LEARN THE TRUTH — READ 'THE LIE'

The book that is sweeping the US and Australia. A powerful message for the layman on what evolution is doing to the church, family and society. Learn why creation matters and what to do about it. Write for order details.

For our free information package. Or if you have any questions on creation or evolution, we'll be happy to offer assistance. We would also like to send you our *free* regular newsletter, to keep you up to date with what is happening in this ministry. Let us know if you would like to receive it. We look forward to hearing from you.

CREATION SCIENCE FOUNDATION LTD,

P.O. Box 302,
Sunnybank, Qld 4109,
Australia.

Phone: (07) 345 8122
Fax: (07) 345 3887